Summer Sizzles

Grilled Recipes to Make the Most of Your Barbecue

CHLOE WOOLERY

informational purposes solely, and is universal as so. The presentation of the information is without contract or any type of guarantee assurance. The trademarks that are used are without any consent, and the publication of the trademark is without permission or backing by the trademark owner. All trademarks and brands within this book are for clarifying purposes only and are the owned by the owners themselves, not affiliated with this document.

Table of Contents

Chapter 1 6

Introduction to Grilling 6

  The History of Grilling................................ 6

  Essential Grilling Equipment 10

  Types of Grills: Charcoal, Gas, and Electric 15

  Grilling Safety Tips 19

  Basic Grilling Techniques........................27

Chapter 2 33

Getting Started 33

  Choosing the Right Grill for You 33

  Setting Up Your Grill 37

  Fuel and Temperature Control........................ 42

  Grill Maintenance and Cleaning.................47

  Common Grilling Mistakes to Avoid 51

Chapter 3 57

Marinades, Rubs, and Sauces 57

  Understanding Flavors: Marinades vs. Rubs.........57

  Creating Your Own Marinades.....................61

  Mastering Dry Rubs................................... 66

  Classic Barbecue Sauces 70

  Innovative Sauces and Glazes 75

  Marinade and Rub Application Tips 80

Chapter 4 86

Grilling Beef... 86

Selecting the Best Cuts of Beef 86

Preparing Beef for the Grill 90

Classic Beef Recipes: Burgers and Steaks 94

Advanced Beef Recipes: Ribs and Brisket............. 98

Beef Cooking Times and Temperature Guide 103

Chapter 1

Introduction to Grilling

The History of Grilling

Grilling is an ancient cooking technique that has evolved significantly over millennia, reflecting cultural shifts, technological advancements, and changing culinary preferences. Its history is a fascinating journey through time, showcasing how humans have adapted and perfected the art of cooking food over an open flame.

The origins of grilling can be traced back to the discovery of fire, approximately 1.8 million years ago. Early humans, such as Homo erectus, began using fire to cook meat, which not only made it more palatable but also easier to digest and safer to eat. This primitive form of grilling likely involved placing meat directly on the flames or hot stones, a method that would lay the foundation for countless grilling techniques to come.

As human societies developed, so did their methods of grilling. The ancient Greeks and Romans were known for their elaborate feasts, often featuring grilled meats. The Greeks, in particular, developed the "kandavlos," a precursor to the modern spit or rotisserie. This device allowed them to cook large pieces of meat evenly over an open flame, a technique that became central to their culinary traditions. The Romans, too, enjoyed grilling and even had portable grills called "craticulae," which they used during military campaigns and public feasts.

Grilling techniques also flourished in other parts of the world. In East Asia, particularly in China and Japan, grilling became an integral part of the culinary landscape. The Chinese developed the "char siu," a method of barbecuing pork with a distinctive sweet and savory glaze. In Japan, "yakitori," skewered and grilled chicken, became a popular street food. These techniques emphasized the importance of marinades and sauces in enhancing the flavor of grilled foods.

The indigenous peoples of the Americas also had rich grilling traditions long before European contact. Native American tribes such as the Taino in the Caribbean developed the "barbacoa," a method of slow-cooking meat over an open flame, which would eventually give rise to the term "barbecue." This method was integral to their way of life, providing a means to preserve meat and infuse it with rich, smoky flavors.

The arrival of Europeans in the New World brought new ingredients and techniques that would further shape the history of grilling. The Spanish introduced cattle, pigs, and chickens to the Americas, which became staples of barbecue culture. In the southern United States, particularly in regions like Texas and the Carolinas, barbecue evolved into a distinct culinary tradition. Each region developed its own styles and preferences, from the vinegar-based sauces of the Carolinas to the beef-centric barbecues of Texas.

The 20th century saw grilling become a beloved pastime in many parts of the world, particularly in the United States. The invention of the charcoal briquette by Henry Ford in the 1920s revolutionized home grilling, making it more accessible to the average person. Charcoal grills became a common feature in American backyards, and grilling became synonymous with family gatherings and summer celebrations.

The post-World War II era saw another significant shift, with the advent of the gas grill in the 1950s. This innovation, credited to Don McGlaughlin, founder of the Chicago Combustion Corporation (later known as LazyMan), made grilling even more convenient. Gas grills allowed for precise temperature control and quicker start-up times, appealing to busy families and expanding the popularity of grilling even further.

In recent decades, grilling has continued to evolve, influenced by global culinary trends and technological advancements. The rise of gourmet grilling has seen chefs experimenting with different woods, marinades, and grilling techniques to create sophisticated and unique flavors. The popularity of international cuisines has also introduced new grilling styles to mainstream audiences, from the Korean "bulgogi" to the South African "braai."

Technological advancements have further transformed grilling. Modern grills come equipped with features such as infrared burners, rotisseries, and smoker boxes, allowing for a wide range of cooking possibilities. Portable grills and tailgating culture have made grilling a popular activity for sports fans and outdoor enthusiasts, while the advent of electric grills has brought the experience indoors, catering to urban dwellers with limited outdoor space.

Despite these advancements, the essence of grilling remains unchanged. It is a communal activity that brings people together, whether around a backyard barbecue, a campsite fire, or a street food stall. The act of grilling transcends cultural boundaries and has a universal appeal, rooted in our primal connection to fire and the simple pleasure of cooking food over an open flame.

The history of grilling is also a testament to human ingenuity and adaptability. From the early discovery of fire to the sophisticated grilling techniques of today, it reflects our constant quest to improve and innovate. Each culture has contributed its unique flavors and methods, enriching the global tapestry of grilling traditions.

As we look to the future, the history of grilling offers valuable insights. It reminds us of the importance of preserving traditional techniques while embracing new innovations. It highlights the role of grilling in fostering community and connection, a role that is perhaps more important than ever in our fast-paced, digital world.

Moreover, the history of grilling underscores the importance of sustainability. As we become more aware of the environmental impact of our food choices, there is a growing movement towards sustainable grilling practices. This includes using eco-friendly fuels, supporting local and ethically sourced ingredients, and reducing waste. By honoring the past while looking to the future, we can ensure that the tradition of grilling continues to thrive for generations to come.

In conclusion, the history of grilling is a rich and varied tapestry, woven from the threads of different cultures, techniques, and innovations. It is a story that spans millennia, reflecting our deep connection to fire and the communal joy of cooking and sharing food. Whether you're a seasoned grill master or a novice just starting out, understanding the history of grilling can deepen your appreciation for this timeless culinary art and inspire you to explore the endless possibilities it offers. As we delve deeper into the history of grilling, it's essential to recognize the regional variations and the cultural significance they hold. Each region's unique methods and flavors are not just culinary choices but also reflect the local environment, available resources, and cultural values.

Essential Grilling Equipment

Grilling is an art that marries simplicity with sophistication, relying on both the right techniques and the right tools. Whether you're a novice griller or an experienced pitmaster, having the essential equipment can make all the difference in your grilling experience. The right tools not only enhance safety and efficiency but also help you achieve the perfect sear, smoke, and flavor in your grilled foods. Here's a comprehensive look at the essential grilling equipment every enthusiast should have.

The cornerstone of any grilling setup is, of course, the grill itself. There are several types of grills, each offering distinct advantages depending on your cooking style and preferences. Charcoal grills, for example, are beloved for the smoky flavor they impart to food. They come in various shapes and sizes, from the classic kettle grill to the versatile kamado grill. The key to using a charcoal grill effectively is learning to control the heat by adjusting the vents and arranging the coals properly. On the other hand, gas grills offer convenience and control, allowing you to adjust the heat with a simple turn of a knob. They heat up quickly and are easy to clean, making them a popular choice for weeknight dinners and larger gatherings. For those who love the taste of wood-fired cooking, pellet grills provide a great option, combining the ease of use of a gas grill with the flavor complexity of a charcoal grill.

Once you have your grill, you'll need a reliable set of grilling tools. A good pair of tongs is indispensable for flipping and moving food without piercing it and losing precious juices. Look for tongs with long handles to keep your hands safely away from the heat, and make sure they have a good grip. A spatula is another must-have, especially for flipping burgers, fish, and other delicate items. Choose one with a wide, thin blade that can easily slide under food. A basting brush is essential for applying marinades and sauces, helping to keep your food moist and flavorful. Silicone brushes are heat-resistant and easy to clean, making them a practical choice.

A meat thermometer is crucial for ensuring your food is cooked to the perfect temperature. Undercooking can pose health risks, while overcooking can ruin the texture and taste of your meal. Instant-read thermometers are a great option for quick checks, while leave-in thermometers can monitor the temperature throughout the cooking process. For larger cuts of meat, a probe thermometer with a remote display can be especially handy, allowing you to monitor the temperature without lifting the grill lid and losing heat.

Grill brushes are essential for maintaining a clean grill. A clean grill not only extends the life of your equipment but also prevents old food residue from affecting the taste of your freshly grilled items. Look for a brush with sturdy bristles that can withstand the rigors of scrubbing grates clean. Some newer models feature replaceable heads or bristles made from materials other than metal to avoid the risk of stray bristles ending up in your food.

For indirect grilling and smoking, a set of grill grates or racks can be very useful. These accessories allow you to cook food at a distance from the direct heat source, perfect for slow-cooking larger cuts of meat or smoking. They also provide additional cooking space, which can be a lifesaver when you're preparing food for a crowd. Some grill models come with adjustable racks, but standalone options are available that fit most standard grills.

A chimney starter is an invaluable tool for charcoal grillers. It allows you to light charcoal quickly and evenly without the need for lighter fluid, which can impart unwanted chemical flavors to your food. Simply fill the chimney with charcoal, place some crumpled newspaper or a fire starter underneath, and light it. In about 15-20 minutes, you'll have perfectly lit coals ready to pour into your grill.

Heat-resistant gloves are a critical safety item for any griller. Handling hot grates, adjusting vents, and moving food can all pose burn risks. Invest in a good pair of gloves that offer both heat resistance and dexterity, allowing you to handle grilling tasks safely and effectively.

For those who enjoy smoking meats, a smoker box is a fantastic addition to your grilling arsenal. This small metal box holds wood chips and fits directly on your grill grates or under them, depending on your grill type. As the wood chips smolder, they produce smoke that infuses your food with rich, smoky flavors. Experiment with different types of wood chips, such as hickory, mesquite, apple, or cherry, to find your favorite flavor combinations.

Drip pans and foil can help keep your grill clean and make indirect grilling easier. Placing a drip pan under your food can catch any drippings, preventing flare-ups and making cleanup simpler. Lining the bottom of your grill or wrapping certain food items in foil can also help manage mess and ensure even cooking.

For the adventurous griller, rotisserie attachments can open up a whole new world of culinary possibilities. Rotisserie cooking allows for even, consistent cooking of larger items like whole chickens, roasts, and even turkeys. The slow rotation ensures that the food bastes in its juices, resulting in tender, flavorful meals.

Additionally, having a solid work surface or prep station near your grill can greatly enhance your grilling experience. This area can be used for food preparation, holding ingredients, and keeping tools within easy reach. Many grills come with side tables, but if yours does not, consider a portable outdoor kitchen cart or table.

Lighting is another often-overlooked aspect of grilling, especially if you enjoy evening cookouts. Ensure your grilling area is well-lit so you can see what you're doing and avoid accidents. Clip-on grill lights or strategically placed outdoor lighting can make a big difference.

Lastly, a good apron with pockets can keep you organized and protect your clothes from splatters and spills. Choose one made from durable, heat-resistant material that is easy to clean.

In summary, while the heart of grilling lies in the joy of cooking over an open flame, having the right equipment can make the process more efficient, safe, and enjoyable. From the grill itself to essential tools like tongs, spatulas, and thermometers, each piece of equipment plays a crucial role in helping you achieve grilling perfection. As you build your collection of grilling gear, consider your specific needs and preferences, and don't be afraid to invest in quality items that will serve you well for years to come. Grilling is as much about the journey as it is about the destination, and having the right tools can make that journey all the more rewarding. Exploring the nuances of essential grilling equipment, it's important to delve into some of the more specialized tools that can elevate your grilling game to new heights. These tools, while not strictly necessary for beginners, can add a level of finesse and versatility that will impress even the most discerning grill aficionados.

Types of Grills: Charcoal, Gas, and Electric

Grilling, an art that transcends cultures and cuisines, hinges on the type of grill you choose. Each type of grill—charcoal, gas, and electric—offers unique advantages and challenges, shaping the flavor, cooking experience, and even the social atmosphere of your grilling sessions. Understanding the nuances of each type can help you decide which grill best suits your needs, whether you're a weekend warrior or a seasoned pitmaster.

Charcoal grills are often heralded as the traditionalist's choice, celebrated for their ability to impart a rich, smoky flavor that is hard to replicate with other types of grills. The process of cooking with charcoal is as much about the journey as it is about the destination. Lighting the coals, waiting for them to reach the perfect temperature, and managing the fire requires patience and skill, but the rewards are well worth the effort.

The most iconic charcoal grill is the kettle grill, originally popularized by Weber. Its simple yet effective design features a round, bowl-like base and a domed lid, which work together to create an ideal environment for both direct and indirect grilling. The key to mastering a kettle grill lies in learning to control the airflow. Vents at the top and bottom of the grill allow you to regulate the temperature, with more air producing a hotter fire and less air cooling things down. By arranging the coals in different configurations, you can create distinct heat zones, perfect for searing steaks on one side and slow-cooking chicken on the other.

For those looking to take their charcoal grilling to the next level, kamado grills offer a versatile and high-performance option. Inspired by ancient Japanese clay cooking vessels, modern kamado grills are typically made from ceramic, which provides excellent heat retention and insulation. This makes them highly efficient and capable of maintaining steady temperatures for extended periods, ideal for low-and-slow cooking techniques like smoking. Kamado grills are also incredibly versatile, capable of grilling, baking, roasting, and smoking with ease.

On the other hand, gas grills are the epitome of convenience in the grilling world. With the simple turn of a knob, you can ignite the burners and start cooking within minutes, making them a popular choice for busy households and impromptu gatherings. Gas grills run on either propane or natural gas, with each fuel source offering its own set of benefits. Propane tanks are portable and widely available, making them a flexible option for those who might want to move their grill around. Natural gas, however, is a more cost-effective and environmentally friendly option, provided you have a natural gas line installed at your home.

Gas grills typically feature multiple burners, which can be adjusted independently to create different cooking zones. This allows for versatile grilling, enabling you to sear a steak over high heat while simultaneously cooking vegetables at a lower temperature. Many gas grills also come equipped with additional features such as side burners, rotisserie attachments, and built-in thermometers, further enhancing their versatility and ease of use.

One of the major advantages of gas grills is their precise temperature control. Unlike charcoal grills, which require constant monitoring and adjustment, gas grills allow you to set and maintain a steady temperature with minimal effort. This makes them particularly well-suited for cooking delicate items like fish or vegetables, which can easily overcook or burn on a less predictable heat source.

Electric grills, the third major type of grill, offer a unique set of benefits that make them an excellent choice for certain situations. Powered by electricity, these grills are incredibly easy to use and require no fuel other than a standard electrical outlet. This makes them a convenient option for apartment dwellers, condo owners, or anyone without access to an outdoor space where charcoal or gas grilling is feasible.

Electric grills come in a variety of shapes and sizes, from compact countertop models to larger freestanding units suitable for outdoor use. Despite their differences in form, all electric grills operate on the same basic principle: heating elements powered by electricity generate the heat needed for cooking. Many electric grills also feature adjustable temperature controls, allowing you to fine-tune the heat to suit whatever you're grilling.

One of the standout features of electric grills is their ability to provide consistent, even heat across the cooking surface. This makes them ideal for grilling items that require a steady temperature, such as chicken breasts, burgers, and vegetables. Additionally, because electric grills do not produce open flames or smoke, they are a safer and cleaner alternative to charcoal or gas grills, particularly in confined spaces.

However, it's worth noting that electric grills typically do not reach the same high temperatures as their charcoal or gas counterparts. This can limit their ability to achieve the same level of searing or charring that many grill enthusiasts crave. Additionally, because they do not use combustion, electric grills lack the distinct smoky flavor imparted by charcoal or even gas grills. Some models come with built-in smoke boxes or wood chip trays to help mimic this flavor, but the results are generally less pronounced.

Choosing the right type of grill ultimately depends on your personal preferences, lifestyle, and grilling goals. If you value the rich, smoky flavor and enjoy the hands-on experience of managing a live fire, a charcoal grill might be the perfect fit. For those who prioritize convenience and precise temperature control, a gas grill offers a versatile and user-friendly option. And if you need a compact, clean, and easy-to-use grill that can be used indoors or in small outdoor spaces, an electric grill is an excellent choice.

Regardless of the type of grill you choose, investing in quality equipment and taking the time to learn its nuances can greatly enhance your grilling experience. Each type of grill has its own unique strengths and can produce delicious results when used correctly. By understanding the fundamental differences between charcoal, gas, and electric grills, you can make an informed decision that best suits your needs and helps you achieve grilling perfection.

In the end, the joy of grilling goes beyond the type of grill you use. It's about the camaraderie of gathering around the fire, the satisfaction of cooking a meal with your own hands, and the pleasure of sharing delicious food with family and friends. Whether you're flipping burgers on a gas grill, smoking ribs on a charcoal grill, or searing veggies on an electric grill, the essence of grilling remains the same: creating memorable meals and moments that bring people together. Understanding the subtleties of each grill type can transform your cooking approach and elevate the flavors you bring to the table. While the choice between charcoal, gas, and electric grills may seem daunting, embracing their unique characteristics can lead to a richer, more rewarding grilling experience. In addition to the fundamental safety tips already discussed, there are several advanced practices and considerations that can further enhance your grilling safety and enjoyment.

Grilling Safety Tips

Grilling is a cherished activity that brings friends and family together over delicious food and good times. However, it also involves handling open flames and high temperatures, which can pose serious safety risks if not managed properly. Ensuring a safe grilling experience requires thorough preparation, careful attention during cooking, and proper procedures for shutting down and cleaning up. By following these grilling safety tips, you can enjoy your cookouts with peace of mind.

Before you even think about lighting the grill, start by choosing a safe location. Place your grill on a flat, stable surface, away from any flammable materials such as wooden structures, dry grass, or overhanging branches. It's essential to position the grill at least ten feet away from your house, garage, or any other building to prevent accidental fires. Additionally, always have a fire extinguisher, a bucket of sand, or a garden hose nearby in case of emergencies.

Inspecting your grill before each use is another crucial step. For gas grills, check the propane tank for leaks by applying a solution of soap and water to the hose and connections. If bubbles form, there's a leak, and the connections should be tightened or replaced. Make sure the burners are clean and free from blockages, which can cause uneven heating or dangerous flare-ups. For charcoal grills, ensure the grill is free from leftover ash or debris from previous uses, as these can obstruct airflow and affect temperature control.

Lighting the grill safely is paramount. For charcoal grills, avoid using lighter fluid or other accelerants, as they can cause uncontrollable flames and impart unpleasant flavors to your food. Instead, use a chimney starter, which allows you to light the charcoal easily and evenly without the need for chemicals. For gas grills, always open the lid before lighting to prevent gas buildup, which can cause an explosion. Follow the manufacturer's instructions for igniting the burners, and never lean over the grill while lighting it.

Once the grill is lit, maintaining a safe cooking environment is key. Keep children and pets away from the grill area to prevent accidental burns or knocks.

Establish a "kid-free zone" of at least three feet around the grill. Use long-handled utensils to avoid getting too close to the heat, and wear heat-resistant gloves to protect your hands. Avoid wearing loose clothing that could catch fire, and tie back long hair.

Managing flare-ups is a critical aspect of grilling safely. Flare-ups occur when fat drips onto the heat source, causing sudden bursts of flame. While they are sometimes unavoidable, they can be controlled. For gas grills, keep a spray bottle of water handy to douse small flare-ups. If a flare-up becomes too intense, move the food to a cooler part of the grill and close the lid to reduce oxygen flow to the flames. For charcoal grills, having a designated cool zone (an area with fewer coals) can help manage flare-ups by providing a place to move the food temporarily.

Monitoring the grill closely is another essential safety practice. Never leave a lit grill unattended, as this increases the risk of accidents. Use a meat thermometer to ensure food is cooked to the proper internal temperature, reducing the risk of foodborne illness. Remember that grilling involves high temperatures, so it's essential to stay vigilant and focused.

Properly extinguishing the grill after use is just as important as lighting it safely. For charcoal grills, allow the coals to burn out completely and cool down before disposing of them. This can take several hours, so plan accordingly. Never dispose of hot coals in a plastic trash can or near flammable materials. Instead, place them in a metal container specifically designed for ash disposal. For gas grills, turn off the burners and the propane tank, then disconnect the tank. Store the propane tank in an upright position outside, away from direct sunlight and heat sources.

Cleaning the grill regularly not only ensures better-tasting food but also significantly reduces the risk of fire. Grease buildup in the grill can ignite, causing dangerous flare-ups. After each use, scrape the grates with a grill brush to remove food particles and grease. Periodically, perform a more thorough cleaning by removing the grates and burners (for gas grills) and cleaning out any accumulated grease and debris from the body of the grill.

While grilling, having a plan for emergencies is essential. If a grease fire occurs, never use water to extinguish it, as this can cause the flames to spread. Instead, cover the grill with its lid to smother the flames and cut off the oxygen supply. If the fire is out of control, use a fire extinguisher rated for grease fires. Familiarize yourself with how to use the extinguisher beforehand, as time is critical during an emergency.

Understanding the impact of weather conditions on grilling safety is also important. Wind can blow sparks and embers onto flammable surfaces, so position your grill in a sheltered area if it's windy. If rain is forecasted, have a safe, covered area where you can move the grill if necessary. Avoid grilling during severe weather conditions, such as thunderstorms, which can pose a significant risk.

Educating yourself and others about grilling safety can make a significant difference. If you often host gatherings where guests may want to help with the grilling, ensure they are aware of these safety practices. Clear communication and established safety protocols can prevent accidents and make for a smoother grilling experience.

Incorporating these safety tips into your grilling routine can greatly reduce the risk of accidents and injuries, allowing you to focus on enjoying the process and the delicious results. Safety should always be a priority, as it ensures that your grilling adventures are not only enjoyable but also incident-free.

Grilling is about more than just cooking food; it's about creating memories with family and friends. By practicing safe grilling habits, you can ensure that these moments are filled with joy and flavor, without the worry of accidents. Embrace the sizzle, the aroma, and the camaraderie, all while keeping safety at the forefront. Whether you're searing steaks, smoking ribs, or grilling vegetables, a safe grilling environment will enhance the experience for everyone involved.

Advanced practices and considerations can further enhance your grilling safety and enjoyment. For instance, consider the importance of grill placement in relation to your surroundings. If you have a deck or patio, ensure that the grill is positioned on a fire-resistant mat to protect the surface underneath from hot embers or grease splatters. If you're grilling in a more confined space, such as a balcony, check the local regulations and building codes to ensure that grilling is permitted and follow any specific guidelines provided.

Be mindful of the fuel you use, particularly with charcoal grills. While natural lump charcoal is often preferred for its cleaner burn and minimal additives, it's crucial to handle it with care. Store charcoal in a dry, cool place to prevent it from absorbing moisture and becoming difficult to ignite. Additionally, never store charcoal or lighter fluid indoors or near heat sources, as they can pose a fire hazard.

For gas grills, regular maintenance of the propane tank and lines is essential for safety. Inspect the tank for any signs of rust or damage, and replace it if necessary. When connecting and disconnecting the tank, ensure that all valves are closed to prevent gas leaks. It's also a good idea to have a professional inspection of your gas grill and tank every few years to ensure everything is in proper working order.

Using grill covers can protect your grill from the elements, but it's important to remove them completely before lighting the grill. Leaving a cover partially on can restrict airflow, leading to poor combustion and increased risk of fire. After grilling, wait until the grill has completely cooled before replacing the cover to avoid trapping heat and moisture, which can damage the grill and create a fire hazard.

Understanding the different types of fires that can occur while grilling and how to handle them is crucial. For instance, grease fires, which are common on grills, require a different approach than other types of fires. Keep a box of baking soda nearby, which can be used to smother small grease fires. For larger fires, a fire extinguisher rated for Class B and K fires (which cover flammable liquids and cooking oils, respectively) is essential.

To avoid cross-contamination while grilling, use separate plates and utensils for raw and cooked foods. Keep raw meat, poultry, and seafood chilled until ready to grill and use a meat thermometer to ensure all foods are cooked to safe internal temperatures. For example, poultry should be cooked to an internal temperature of 165°F (74°C), while ground meats should reach 160°F (71°C).

Hydration and sun protection are often overlooked aspects of grilling safety. If you're grilling outdoors on a hot day, take measures to stay hydrated and protect yourself from the sun. Wear a hat, apply sunscreen, and take breaks in the shade to avoid heat exhaustion or sunburn. Drinking plenty of water is essential to stay hydrated, especially if you're consuming alcoholic beverages, which can dehydrate you.

For those who enjoy grilling with wood chips or chunks for added flavor, use them safely. Soak the wood chips in water for at least 30 minutes before placing them on the coals or in a smoker box to prevent them from catching fire too quickly. Monitor the smoke levels and adjust the vents to maintain a controlled smoke flow, ensuring the food gets the desired flavor without excessive smoke, which can be harmful if inhaled.

If you're planning to grill in a public area, such as a park or campsite, follow all local regulations and guidelines. Use designated grilling areas and dispose of charcoal and other waste properly. Never leave a lit grill unattended in a public space, and be mindful of the environment by preventing litter and ensuring your grill doesn't damage the surrounding area.

For those who enjoy experimenting with different grilling techniques, such as rotisserie cooking or smoking, additional safety measures are needed. When using a rotisserie, ensure it is securely fastened to prevent it from tipping over or the meat from falling off. If you're using a smoker, maintain consistent temperatures and avoid opening the lid too frequently, which can cause temperature fluctuations and increase the risk of flare-ups.

Don't underestimate the importance of education and staying informed. Taking a grilling safety course or reading up on the latest safety guidelines can provide valuable knowledge and skills. Many local fire departments and community centers offer grilling safety workshops, which can be an excellent resource for both beginners and experienced grillers.

Grilling is a wonderful way to enjoy food and spend time outdoors, but it comes with responsibilities. By following these advanced safety tips and continuously educating yourself, you can minimize risks and enjoy a safe, pleasant grilling experience. Whether you're cooking a simple weeknight dinner or hosting a large barbecue, prioritizing safety ensures that your time spent grilling is both enjoyable and uneventful.

In conclusion, grilling safety encompasses a wide range of practices, from proper grill placement and fuel handling to managing flare-ups and preventing cross-contamination. By integrating these tips into your routine, you can create a safe environment that allows you to focus on the joy of grilling and the delicious food it produces. Always stay vigilant, prepared, and informed to ensure that every grilling session is a success. In addition to the practical tips and advanced considerations already discussed, understanding the nuances of different grilling scenarios can further enhance safety and enjoyment. Whether you're a weekend warrior or a seasoned pit master, adapting your approach to various situations can make all the difference.

Basic Grilling Techniques

Grilling is an art that balances heat, timing, and flavor. Understanding the foundational techniques is essential for any novice griller eager to master the craft. This chapter delves into the basics, providing a solid foundation upon which you can build more advanced skills.

The first step in grilling is selecting the right grill for your needs. Charcoal grills offer a distinct smoky flavor and the ability to reach high temperatures, ideal for searing. Gas grills provide convenience, with easy temperature control and quick start-up times. Electric grills, while less traditional, are excellent for indoor use or in areas with strict fire regulations. Each type of grill has its pros and cons, and your choice will depend on your personal preferences and living situation.

Once you've chosen your grill, proper setup is crucial. For charcoal grills, arrange the coals in a pyramid shape and use a chimney starter or lighter fluid to ignite them. Allow the coals to burn until they are covered with a light layer of ash, indicating they are ready for cooking. Gas grills should be preheated with all burners on high for about 10-15 minutes. This preheating step is vital as it ensures the grill reaches the desired temperature and helps to clean the grates.

Cleaning your grill grates before and after use is a fundamental practice. Use a grill brush to remove any residual food particles and debris. This not only prevents unwanted flavors from contaminating your food but also reduces the risk of flare-ups caused by grease buildup. For a deeper clean, occasionally remove the grates and soak them in warm, soapy water.

One of the most essential grilling techniques is creating direct and indirect heat zones. Direct heat is achieved by placing food directly over the heat source, which is perfect for searing and cooking thinner cuts of meat or vegetables quickly. Indirect heat involves placing food away from the heat source, allowing it to cook more slowly and evenly, which is ideal for thicker cuts of meat, whole chickens, or roasts. On a charcoal grill, this is done by arranging the coals to one side or in a ring around the perimeter. On a gas grill, simply turn off one or more burners to create a cooler zone.

Temperature control is another critical aspect of successful grilling. Invest in a good-quality meat thermometer to ensure your food reaches the desired internal temperature. For example, chicken should reach an internal temperature of 165°F, while medium-rare beef is best at 135°F. Additionally, learning to gauge the grill's temperature by feel can be a useful skill. Hold your hand about five inches above the grill grates. If you can only hold it there for 1-2 seconds, the grill is on high heat; 3-4 seconds indicates medium heat, and 5-6 seconds means low heat.

Marinades and rubs are excellent ways to infuse flavor into your grilled dishes. Marinades typically consist of an acidic component such as vinegar or citrus juice, oil, and various herbs and spices. They help tenderize the meat and impart flavor. However, avoid marinating delicate proteins like fish for too long, as the acid can break down the flesh. Dry rubs, on the other hand, are mixtures of spices and herbs that are rubbed directly onto the meat's surface. They create a flavorful crust when grilled and are especially effective on cuts like ribs or brisket.

One common mistake beginners make is constantly flipping and moving the food on the grill. Resist this urge. Allowing the food to cook undisturbed for several minutes forms a nice crust and ensures even cooking. When grilling steaks, for example, flip them only once to achieve the perfect sear. The same principle applies to burgers and chicken breasts.

Resting your meat after grilling is a crucial step that should not be overlooked. Allowing the meat to rest for 5-10 minutes after removing it from the grill enables the juices to redistribute throughout the meat, resulting in a juicier and more flavorful dish. Cover the meat loosely with aluminum foil to keep it warm while it rests.

Grilling vegetables requires a slightly different approach than grilling meat. Vegetables benefit from a light coating of oil to prevent sticking and promote even charring. Some vegetables, like bell peppers, zucchini, and asparagus, grill well directly on the grates. Others, like cherry tomatoes or smaller pieces, are best cooked in a grill basket to prevent them from falling through the grates. Keep a close eye on vegetables, as they cook quickly and can easily become overdone.

Safety is paramount when grilling. Always keep a spray bottle of water nearby to manage flare-ups, which occur when fat drips onto the heat source and ignites. Never leave a lit grill unattended, and keep children and pets at a safe distance. For gas grills, regularly check the propane tank and hoses for leaks by applying a soapy water solution; bubbles indicate a leak that needs immediate attention.

Using a lid while grilling can significantly impact the cooking process. Closing the lid traps heat and smoke, which helps cook food evenly and imparts a smoky flavor. This technique is especially beneficial for thicker cuts of meat and larger items like whole chickens or roasts. Conversely, grilling with the lid open is suitable for quick-cooking items like burgers, hot dogs, and vegetables, where you want a good sear without overcooking the interior.

Experimenting with different types of wood chips can add a unique smoky flavor to your grilled dishes. Wood chips come in various flavors, such as hickory, mesquite, apple, and cherry. Soak the wood chips in water for at least 30 minutes before adding them to the coals or placing them in a smoker box on a gas grill. Each type of wood imparts a distinct flavor, with fruitwoods offering a milder, sweeter smoke and hardwoods providing a stronger, more robust taste.

Grilling isn't just limited to traditional meats and vegetables. Expanding your repertoire to include items like pizza, fruit, and even desserts can elevate your grilling game. Grilled pizza, for instance, develops a wonderfully crispy crust with a slightly smoky flavor. Simply roll out the dough, brush it with olive oil, and grill it until bubbly before adding your favorite toppings. Grilled fruits like peaches, pineapples, and watermelon caramelize beautifully and pair well with savory dishes or can be served as a dessert with a scoop of ice cream.

Understanding when to use certain grilling tools can also enhance your experience. Long-handled tongs are essential for turning meat without piercing it and releasing juices. A spatula is useful for flipping more delicate items like fish fillets or burgers. Basting brushes come in handy for applying marinades or sauces, and skewers are perfect for kebabs. Opt for metal skewers over wooden ones, as they are reusable and don't require soaking.

Finally, the key to becoming proficient at grilling is practice and patience. Start with simple recipes and gradually work your way up to more complex dishes. Don't be afraid to make mistakes; they are part of the learning process. Pay attention to how different foods react to various heat levels and cooking times. Over time, you'll develop a sense of intuition that will guide you in creating delicious grilled meals with confidence.

Embracing these basic grilling techniques will set you on the path to becoming a skilled griller. From selecting the right grill and setting up your cooking zones to mastering temperature control and experimenting with flavors, these foundational practices are the building blocks of grilling excellence. With dedication and practice, you'll soon be able to impress your friends and family with perfectly grilled dishes every time. As you continue to hone your grilling skills, it's important to experiment and adapt. Every grill is different, and so is every piece of meat or vegetable you cook. Variations in thickness, fat content, and moisture levels can all affect cooking times and the final result. Paying close attention to these details will help you make real-time adjustments and avoid common pitfalls.

Chapter 2

Getting Started

Choosing the Right Grill for You

Choosing the right grill is a fundamental step in your journey to becoming a proficient griller. The myriad options available can be overwhelming, but understanding the characteristics, benefits, and drawbacks of each type will help you make an informed decision tailored to your needs and preferences.

Begin by considering where you'll be grilling most often. If you live in an apartment or a place with strict fire regulations, an electric grill might be your best option. These grills are compact, can be used indoors, and don't produce open flames, making them a safe choice for confined spaces. However, they lack the smoky flavor that comes from burning wood or charcoal, which is a significant consideration for many grilling enthusiasts.

For those with more outdoor space, the choice often comes down to gas or charcoal grills. Gas grills are popular for their convenience and ease of use. They ignite quickly, typically with the push of a button, and allow for precise temperature control, much like an indoor stove. This makes them ideal for those who want to grill frequently and with minimal fuss. Additionally, gas grills often come with multiple burners, providing the flexibility to create different heat zones for cooking various foods simultaneously.

Some advanced models even include side burners, rotisserie attachments, and smoker boxes, expanding your culinary capabilities.

Charcoal grills, on the other hand, are beloved for the rich, smoky flavor they impart to food. The process of lighting the coals and waiting for them to reach the right temperature can be time-consuming, but many grillers find this ritual part of the joy of grilling. Charcoal grills can achieve higher temperatures than gas grills, making them excellent for searing meats and achieving that perfect crust. They also tend to be more portable, as they don't require a gas hookup, making them a favorite for tailgating and camping trips. However, controlling the temperature on a charcoal grill requires more skill and practice, as it involves adjusting the air vents and managing the coals.

Another type of grill gaining popularity is the pellet grill. These grills use wood pellets as fuel, combining the convenience of gas grills with the flavor of charcoal grills. Pellet grills are equipped with digital controllers that maintain a set temperature, feeding pellets into the fire as needed. This makes them highly versatile, capable of low-and-slow smoking as well as high-heat grilling. However, they tend to be more expensive than other types of grills and require a power source to operate the digital components.

Kamado grills, such as the Big Green Egg, represent another option for those seeking versatility and superior heat retention. Made from ceramic, these grills can maintain steady temperatures for long periods, making them excellent for smoking as well as grilling and baking. Their design allows for precise control over airflow and temperature, but they are typically heavier and more expensive than traditional charcoal grills.

Portability might also be a crucial factor in your decision. If you enjoy camping, picnicking, or tailgating, a portable grill could be the perfect choice. These grills come in both gas and charcoal varieties and are designed to be lightweight and easy to transport. While they may not offer the same cooking space or features as larger grills, they are convenient for on-the-go grilling.

Consider your budget when choosing a grill. While it's tempting to go for the model with all the bells and whistles, it's important to find a grill that fits within your financial constraints. Entry-level models can provide excellent performance at a fraction of the cost of high-end grills. However, investing in a quality grill can save you money in the long run, as cheaper models may need to be replaced more frequently.

Think about the types of food you plan to grill. If you enjoy a variety of grilled dishes, from steaks and burgers to fish and vegetables, a versatile grill with adjustable temperature zones and multiple cooking surfaces will serve you well. For those who primarily grill meats, a charcoal grill or a gas grill with searing capabilities might be more appropriate.

Maintenance and ease of cleaning are other important considerations. Gas grills generally require less cleanup than charcoal grills, as they produce fewer ashes. Look for grills with removable drip trays and grates that are easy to clean. Some models come with self-cleaning features, such as grease management systems, which can save you time and effort.

The material and construction of the grill are also critical factors. Stainless steel grills are durable, resistant to rust, and often more attractive, but they can be more expensive. Cast iron grates retain heat well and create excellent grill marks, but they require regular seasoning to prevent rust. Porcelain-coated grates offer a non-stick surface and are easier to clean, but they can chip over time.

Consider the fuel source and availability. Gas grills can be connected to a natural gas line or use propane tanks. Make sure you have easy access to refill or replace your propane tanks or connect to a natural gas source if you choose a gas grill. Charcoal grills require a steady supply of charcoal and possibly wood chips for smoking, so factor in the cost and storage of these materials.

Safety features should not be overlooked. Look for grills with sturdy construction, stable bases, and lids that fit securely. Gas grills should have reliable ignition systems and flame tamers to prevent flare-ups. Charcoal grills should have vents and dampers that are easy to adjust and stay cool to the touch.

Once you've considered all these factors, it's beneficial to read reviews and seek recommendations. Online reviews can provide insights into the performance and durability of different models. Visiting a store to see the grills in person and speaking with knowledgeable salespeople can also help you make a final decision.

Choosing the right grill is a personal decision that depends on various factors, including your living situation, budget, and grilling preferences. Whether you opt for the convenience of a gas grill, the flavor of a charcoal grill, the versatility of a pellet grill, or the heat retention of a komodo grill, understanding the features and benefits of each type will help you make an informed choice. With the right grill, you'll be well on your way to creating delicious grilled dishes and enjoying the many pleasures of outdoor cooking. Once you've selected the right grill, it's time to set it up and get acquainted with its features. For gas grills, ensure all connections are secure and check for any gas leaks before using it for the first time. This typically involves applying a soapy water solution to the connections and looking for bubbles, which indicate a leak. For charcoal grills, assemble the components according to the manufacturer's instructions and familiarize yourself with the ventilation system, as proper airflow is crucial for maintaining consistent temperatures.

Setting Up Your Grill

Setting up your grill is an essential step that sets the stage for all your future culinary adventures. Whether you've chosen a gas, charcoal, pellet, or kamado grill, proper setup ensures safety, efficiency, and optimal performance. This chapter will guide you through the process of setting up various types of grills, providing practical tips and insights to help you get started.

The first step in setting up your grill is selecting an appropriate location. Ideally, your grill should be placed on a flat, stable surface away from any flammable materials such as wooden decks, dry leaves, or overhanging branches. Ensure there is enough clearance around the grill to allow for proper ventilation and safe operation. If using a gas grill, make sure it is positioned near a gas supply line or that you have easy access to propane tanks. For charcoal and pellet grills, consider proximity to storage areas for your fuel sources.

Once you've identified the perfect spot, it's time to assemble your grill. Start by unpacking all the components and reviewing the manufacturer's instructions. While assembly processes vary depending on the type and model of grill, the general steps are similar. Begin with the base and frame, ensuring all screws and bolts are securely tightened. Attach any shelves, side tables, and other accessories according to the instructions. For gas grills, connect the burners and ignition system, making sure all connections are secure and free from leaks. Pellet grills may require the installation of a hopper and auger system, while kamado grills typically involve assembling the ceramic components and attaching the vent systems.

After assembling your grill, perform a thorough inspection to ensure everything is correctly installed and functioning properly. For gas grills, this includes checking the gas lines and connections for leaks. One common method is to apply a soapy water solution to the connections and look for bubbles, which indicate escaping gas. Tighten any loose connections and repeat the test until no bubbles appear. For charcoal and pellet grills, check that all vents and dampers open and close smoothly, and that the grates are securely in place.

Before using your grill for the first time, it's important to season it. Seasoning helps to remove any manufacturing residues and creates a protective layer on the grates, reducing the likelihood of rust and improving the grill's non-stick properties. For gas grills, preheat the grill on high for about 15 minutes, then brush the grates with oil using a high smoke point oil such as canola or grapeseed oil. For charcoal and pellet grills, light a small amount of fuel and let the grill heat up to high temperatures for a similar duration before applying oil to the grates. Kamado grills, with their ceramic surfaces, may not require seasoning, but it's always best to consult the manufacturer's guidelines.

With your grill seasoned and ready, consider the tools and accessories that will enhance your grilling experience. Essential tools include long-handled tongs, spatulas, and basting brushes, which allow you to handle food safely over high heat. A meat thermometer is crucial for ensuring meats are cooked to the correct internal temperatures, while grill brushes and scrapers help keep the grates clean. For gas grills, additional accessories such as smoker boxes, rotisserie kits, and grill mats can expand your cooking capabilities. Charcoal grill users might benefit from chimney starters for easy coal ignition, while pellet grill enthusiasts could look into pellet storage containers and cleaning kits. Kamado grill users might invest in heat deflectors and pizza stones to diversify their cooking techniques.

Understanding how to properly light your grill is key to successful grilling. Gas grills are the easiest to ignite; simply open the lid, turn on the gas supply, and use the ignition button or lighter to start the burners. Allow the grill to preheat for at least ten minutes before cooking. For charcoal grills, use a chimney starter filled with charcoal briquettes or lump charcoal. Light a fire starter or crumpled newspaper at the bottom of the chimney starter and let the coals ignite. Once the coals are ashed over, carefully pour them into the grill and arrange them according to your cooking needs. Pellet grills often feature automatic ignition systems; fill the hopper with pellets, set your desired temperature on the digital controller, and let the grill do the rest. Kamado grills require a small amount of lump charcoal and a fire starter; light the starter, leave the lid open until the coals are well-lit, then close the lid and adjust the vents to reach your desired temperature.

Temperature control is crucial for grilling success. Gas grills offer precise temperature control through adjustable burners, allowing you to create different heat zones for direct and indirect cooking. Charcoal grills require more practice; control the temperature by adjusting the air vents and the amount of charcoal. Spread the coals out evenly for high heat, or bank them to one side for indirect cooking. Pellet grills maintain consistent temperatures through their digital controllers, though you can fine-tune the heat by adjusting the pellet feed rate. Kamado grills excel at temperature control due to their insulated ceramic walls; use the top and bottom vents to regulate airflow and maintain steady temperatures.

Cleaning and maintenance are vital for the longevity and performance of your grill. After each use, allow the grill to cool slightly, then brush the grates to remove any food debris. For gas grills, periodically check the burners for clogs and ensure the grease tray is emptied regularly. Charcoal grills should have ash removed after each use to prevent buildup, which can obstruct airflow. Pellet grills require regular cleaning of the fire pot and hopper to ensure efficient operation. Kamado grills benefit from occasional deep cleaning to remove grease and ash from the ceramic surfaces.

Regularly inspect your grill for signs of wear and tear. Gas grills should have their hoses and connections checked for leaks or cracks. Charcoal and pellet grills should have their vents and grates inspected for rust or damage. Kamado grills, due to their ceramic nature, should be checked for cracks or chips, and any damaged components should be replaced promptly.

Finally, investing in a good grill cover will protect your grill from the elements and prolong its life. Make sure the cover fits snugly and is made from durable, weather-resistant material. Store your grill in a sheltered area during extreme weather conditions to prevent damage.

Setting up your grill properly lays the foundation for all your grilling endeavors. By following these steps, you'll ensure your grill operates safely and efficiently, allowing you to focus on creating delicious meals and enjoying the art of grilling. As you become more familiar with your grill, you'll gain confidence in your abilities and develop your own techniques and preferences, making each grilling session a rewarding experience. As you continue to hone your grilling skills, it's important to understand the nuances of maintaining consistent temperatures and managing your fuel sources effectively. For gas grills, this might involve mastering the use of each burner to create different heat zones. For instance, you can keep one burner on high to sear meats and another on low to cook vegetables slowly. Periodic checks of the propane tank's levels will prevent unexpected interruptions during your cooking sessions.

Fuel and Temperature Control

Mastering fuel and temperature control is a pivotal skill in the art of grilling. These elements are the backbone of your grilling success, dictating everything from the flavor profile of your food to the efficiency of your cooking process. Whether you're using a gas, charcoal, pellet, or kamado grill, understanding how to manage fuel and control temperature will elevate your grilling game to new heights.

For gas grills, fuel management is relatively straightforward, as propane or natural gas provides a consistent and easily adjustable heat source. The key to mastering temperature control with a gas grill lies in understanding your grill's burner system and how to create different heat zones. Most gas grills come equipped with multiple burners, allowing you to set up direct and indirect heat zones. Direct heat is ideal for searing steaks or grilling vegetables quickly, while indirect heat is perfect for slow-cooking larger cuts of meat or delicate items that require gentle, even cooking.

Start by preheating your grill with all burners on high. This not only ensures that the grates are hot enough to sear food properly but also helps burn off any residual debris from previous cooking sessions. Once the grill is preheated, adjust the burners to create the desired heat zones. For example, if you're cooking a thick steak, you might set one burner to high for searing and another to medium-low for finishing the steak without burning the outside. Monitoring the internal temperature of your grill with a built-in or standalone thermometer is crucial to maintaining consistent heat levels.

Charcoal grills, while offering unparalleled flavor, require a more hands-on approach to fuel and temperature management. The type and amount of charcoal you use, as well as how you arrange it, significantly impact your cooking results. Lump charcoal burns hotter and faster than briquettes, making it ideal for high-heat grilling and quick searing. Briquettes, on the other hand, provide a more consistent and longer-lasting heat, which is beneficial for slow-cooking and smoking.

To achieve optimal temperature control with a charcoal grill, start by using a chimney starter to light the coals. This method ensures even ignition and reduces the need for lighter fluid, which can impart unwanted flavors to your food. Once the coals are ashed over, you can arrange them in different configurations depending on your cooking needs. For high-heat grilling, spread the coals in an even layer across the bottom of the grill. For indirect cooking, bank the coals to one side or create a two-zone setup with coals on one half of the grill and an empty space on the other.

Adjusting the grill's vents is another critical aspect of temperature control. The bottom vents control the amount of oxygen entering the grill, while the top vents regulate the flow of hot air and smoke. Opening the vents increases the temperature by allowing more oxygen to fuel the fire, while closing them reduces the temperature. It's a delicate balance that requires practice and attention, but mastering vent control will enable you to maintain steady temperatures for extended cooking sessions.

Pellet grills combine the convenience of gas grills with the flavor benefits of charcoal, using compressed wood pellets as fuel. These grills feature a hopper that feeds pellets into a fire pot, where they are ignited to produce heat and smoke. The temperature is controlled by a digital controller, which regulates the pellet feed rate and airflow. This automated system makes it easier to maintain precise temperatures, but understanding the nuances of pellet types and their burning characteristics is still essential.

Different wood pellets impart different flavors, so selecting the right type of pellet is crucial for achieving the desired taste. Hickory and mesquite pellets provide strong, smoky flavors suitable for robust meats like beef and pork, while fruitwood pellets like apple and cherry offer milder, sweeter notes perfect for poultry and fish. Regularly cleaning the fire pot and ensuring the auger feeds pellets smoothly will prevent temperature fluctuations and maintain consistent cooking conditions.

Kamado grills, known for their versatility and superior heat retention, require a unique approach to fuel and temperature control. These ceramic grills use lump charcoal, which burns hotter and cleaner than briquettes. The thick, insulated walls of a kamado grill help maintain steady temperatures for long periods, making them ideal for both high-heat grilling and low-and-slow smoking.

To light a kamado grill, place a small amount of lump charcoal in the firebox and use a fire starter to ignite it. Leave the lid open until the coals are well-lit, then close the lid and adjust the vents to control the temperature. The bottom vent allows air to enter the grill, while the top vent controls the exhaust. For high-heat cooking, open both vents fully to maximize airflow. For low-and-slow cooking, close the vents slightly to reduce the oxygen supply and lower the temperature. The ceramic construction of a kamado grill allows for precise temperature adjustments, but it's important to make changes gradually and monitor the internal temperature closely.

Regardless of the type of grill you use, maintaining consistent temperatures is essential for achieving perfect results. One of the most effective ways to monitor and control temperature is by using a reliable thermometer. Built-in thermometers can give you a general idea of the grill's internal temperature, but they often have inaccuracies. Investing in a high-quality digital thermometer with a probe that can be placed at grate level will provide more accurate readings. This is especially important for smoking and slow-cooking, where precise temperature control is crucial.

Managing fuel and temperature control also involves understanding how different weather conditions can impact your grilling. Wind, rain, and cold temperatures can affect how your grill performs. Wind can increase the oxygen supply and raise the temperature in charcoal grills, while cold weather may require you to use more fuel to maintain the same heat levels. Being aware of these factors and adjusting your grill settings accordingly will help you achieve consistent results, regardless of the weather.

Another aspect of temperature control is knowing when and how to use the lid of your grill. Keeping the lid closed helps retain heat and smoke, creating a convection effect that cooks food evenly. However, opening the lid frequently can cause temperature fluctuations, so it's important to minimize lid openings and monitor the cooking process through the thermometer instead of constantly checking the food.

Lastly, understanding the concept of carryover cooking is crucial for achieving perfect doneness. When you remove food from the grill, it continues to cook for a few minutes due to residual heat. This is especially important for thick cuts of meat, where the internal temperature can rise by several degrees after being taken off the grill. To account for carryover cooking, remove the food from the grill when it's a few degrees below the target temperature, and let it rest for a few minutes before serving.

Fuel and temperature control are the cornerstones of successful grilling. Mastering these elements requires practice, patience, and a keen understanding of your specific grill. By learning how to manage fuel sources, adjust vents, and monitor temperatures accurately, you'll be well on your way to becoming a grilling expert. The ability to control heat and fuel not only ensures perfectly cooked food but also allows you to explore a wide range of grilling techniques and recipes, making your culinary journey both exciting and rewarding. Experimenting with different fuel types and temperature settings can also lead to delightful culinary discoveries. For instance, blending different wood chips can create unique flavors. A mix of hickory and Applewood might yield a balanced smoky-sweet profile perfect for pork ribs. Similarly, playing with temperature settings can help you find the sweet spot for various dishes. Low-and-slow cooking at 225°F can result in tender, juicy pulled pork, while a higher temperature of 375°F might be ideal for crispy-skinned chicken.

Grill Maintenance and Cleaning

Regular grill maintenance and cleaning are essential practices that should be embraced by every griller. Not only do they prolong the life of your grill, but they also ensure that every meal you cook is safe, flavorful, and free from undesirable residues. Proper upkeep can seem daunting, but with a few straightforward steps and a bit of diligence, your grill can remain in peak condition for years to come.

Cleaning your grill after every use is the first and most crucial step in maintaining it. Begin by preheating the grill on high for about 10-15 minutes. This step burns off any remaining food particles and makes subsequent cleaning easier. Once the grill has cooled to a safe temperature, use a high-quality grill brush to scrub the grates. Stainless steel or brass-bristled brushes are recommended because they effectively remove debris without damaging the grill surface. Make sure to brush in the direction of the grates to dislodge any stuck-on food.

For gas grills, focus not only on the grates but also on the burner protectors and the burners themselves. Burner protectors, or heat deflectors, can accumulate grease and food particles, which can cause flare-ups. Remove these protectors and scrub them thoroughly. Check the burners for clogs or debris, using a wire brush or a specialized burner cleaning brush to clear any blockages. Ensuring the burners are clean and unobstructed is vital for even gas flow and consistent heat distribution.

Charcoal grills require a different approach. After each use, make sure to remove and dispose of the ash. Ash can trap moisture, leading to rust and corrosion if left for extended periods. Many charcoal grills come with an ash catcher, which makes this process easier. If yours doesn't, use a small shovel or scoop to clear out the ash. Once the ash is removed, inspect the grill grates and the interior of the grill for any remaining debris and clean them accordingly.

Deep cleaning your grill is necessary at least once a season, or more frequently if you use it often. Start by disassembling the grill to access all its components. Remove the grates, burner protectors, and any other removable parts. Soak these items in a solution of warm water and mild dish soap. While they soak, use a putty knife or grill scraper to remove built-up grease and carbon from the grill's interior surfaces. Pay special attention to the sides, bottom, and hood of the grill.

For stubborn grime, consider using a grill-specific degreaser or a mixture of baking soda and water. Apply the cleaner to the affected areas, let it sit for a few minutes, then scrub with a non-abrasive pad. Rinse all parts thoroughly with water to remove any soap residue, and allow them to dry completely before reassembling the grill.

Maintaining the exterior of your grill is just as important as the interior. Stainless steel grills are prone to fingerprints and smudges, so regular wiping with a stainless steel cleaner or a mixture of vinegar and water will keep them looking pristine. For painted surfaces, use a mild detergent and water. Avoid abrasive cleaners or scouring pads, as they can scratch and damage the finish.

Protecting your grill from the elements is another key aspect of maintenance. Investing in a high-quality grill cover is one of the best ways to shield your grill from rain, snow, and UV rays. Choose a cover that fits your grill snugly and is made from durable, weather-resistant materials. Using a cover not only extends the life of your grill but also reduces the frequency of cleanings required.

Inspecting your grill for wear and tear should be part of your routine maintenance. Check for signs of rust, particularly on the grates, burners, and any exposed metal parts. If you notice rust spots, treat them promptly with a wire brush and a rust remover. For more severe rusting, consider replacing the affected parts. Regularly check hoses and connections on gas grills for leaks or cracks. A simple soapy water solution can help identify gas leaks—if you see bubbles forming when the gas is turned on, you have a leak that needs immediate attention.

Lubricating moving parts, such as hinges and wheels, ensures smooth operation and prevents squeaking. Use a high-temperature lubricant or cooking oil to keep these parts functioning properly. If your grill has a built-in ignition system, periodically check the batteries and replace them as needed to avoid any surprise failures during cooking.

Another aspect of grill maintenance is proper storage during the off-season. If you live in an area with harsh winters, consider storing your grill in a garage or shed to protect it from extreme weather. If indoor storage isn't an option, make sure your grill is thoroughly cleaned and covered. Disconnect and store the propane tank separately in a safe, well-ventilated area.

For charcoal grills, it's a good practice to remove any remaining charcoal and clean the grill thoroughly before storing it. This prevents moisture from mixing with the ash and causing rust. For gas grills, shut off the gas supply and disconnect the propane tank. Store the tank in a secure, cool place, away from any potential sources of ignition.

Regularly servicing your grill can also prevent minor issues from becoming major problems. Many manufacturers offer service packages or can recommend certified technicians to perform annual maintenance checks. These professionals can inspect and clean components you might overlook, ensuring your grill operates at peak performance.

Grill maintenance and cleaning might seem like a chore, but it's a small price to pay for the benefits they provide. A well-maintained grill not only performs better but also enhances the safety and quality of your cooking. By incorporating these practices into your grilling routine, you'll enjoy consistently delicious food and extend the life of your grill, making every cookout a memorable event.

Remember, the time and effort you invest in maintaining your grill will pay off in the long run. Not only will you avoid costly repairs and replacements, but you'll also ensure that your grill is always ready to fire up for your next culinary adventure. Whether you're a seasoned griller or a novice, taking care of your equipment is a fundamental part of the grilling experience. Embrace the process, and you'll find that a clean, well-maintained grill is one of the best tools you can have in your culinary arsenal. A little attention to detail goes a long way in grill maintenance. Keep a simple maintenance schedule, jotting down dates of deep cleanings, part replacements, and inspections. This log will help you stay on top of necessary upkeep tasks, preventing small issues from snowballing into larger problems.

Common Grilling Mistakes to Avoid

Grilling is an art that combines technique, timing, and a touch of intuition. However, even the most seasoned grill masters can fall into some common pitfalls. Avoiding these mistakes can significantly enhance your grilling experience and the quality of your food.

Let's dive into the most frequent grilling errors and how to sidestep them for consistently delicious results.

One of the most prevalent mistakes is not preheating the grill properly. Firing up the grill and immediately placing food on it might seem efficient, but it leads to uneven cooking and poor sear marks. Always preheat your grill for at least 15 minutes before adding any food. This ensures that the grates are hot enough to create those desirable grill marks and helps to cook the food evenly. A well-preheated grill also prevents food from sticking to the grates.

Using the wrong type of fuel can drastically affect the taste and cooking process. For instance, using lighter fluid on charcoal can impart a chemical taste to your food. Instead, use a chimney starter to light charcoal briquettes or lump charcoal. This method is not only safer but also preserves the natural flavor of the food. For gas grills, ensure you're using the appropriate type of propane or natural gas, and regularly check for leaks to maintain safety and efficiency.

Overcrowding the grill is another common issue. While it might be tempting to maximize the space, overcrowding can lead to uneven cooking and flare-ups. Each piece of food needs ample space for heat to circulate and cook it properly. When the grill is too crowded, the temperature drops, and food can end up steamed rather than grilled, resulting in a loss of texture and flavor. Cook in batches if necessary, allowing each item enough room to breathe.

Flipping food too frequently is a mistake many novices make. Constantly turning meat or vegetables prevents them from developing a proper sear and can lead to sticking. Patience is key when grilling. Let the food cook undisturbed until it naturally releases from the grates, then flip it. Generally, flipping meat once is sufficient, ensuring a beautiful crust forms on each side.

Using sugary marinades too early in the cooking process can cause charring. While marinades and glazes add wonderful flavors, those with high sugar content can burn quickly over high heat. Apply these during the last few minutes of cooking to avoid a charred and bitter taste. Alternatively, you can marinate the food for a few hours beforehand and pat it dry before grilling, then add a glaze towards the end.

Neglecting to clean the grill grates before and after cooking is a significant oversight. Dirty grates not only affect the taste of your food but also pose a health risk due to the buildup of grease and charred residue. A clean grill ensures better flavor and reduces the likelihood of flare-ups. After preheating the grill, use a grill brush to scrape off any residual debris. Post-cooking, once the grill has cooled slightly, another quick brush will prepare it for the next use.

Failing to use a meat thermometer can result in undercooked or overcooked food. Guessing doneness based on time alone is unreliable because various factors, such as grill temperature and food thickness, influence cooking time. A meat thermometer takes the guesswork out of grilling, ensuring your food reaches the safe internal temperature for consumption. For instance, poultry should reach 165°F, while medium-rare beef is perfect at 135°F.

Another frequent mistake is not allowing meat to rest after cooking. Slicing into meat immediately after removing it from the grill causes the juices to escape, resulting in dry, less flavorful food. Letting meat rest for a few minutes allows the juices to redistribute, ensuring every bite is moist and delicious. For larger cuts, like brisket or roasts, resting for up to 15 minutes can make a substantial difference.

Improperly handling flare-ups can ruin your grilling experience and your food. Flare-ups happen when fat drips onto the heat source, causing flames to rise. While some flare-ups are inevitable, controlling them is crucial. Keep a spray bottle of water handy to douse small flames. For more significant flare-ups, move the food to a cooler section of the grill until the flames subside. Avoid using water excessively on gas grills, as it can cause damage.

Ignoring the importance of indirect heat is another common error. Direct heat is excellent for searing, but not all foods benefit from this method throughout the cooking process. Larger cuts of meat, like whole chickens or ribs, cook better with indirect heat, which prevents the exterior from burning before the interior is properly cooked. Learn to manage your grill's zones, using direct heat for searing and indirect heat for slow cooking.

Using the wrong tools can also hinder your grilling success. Investing in quality grill tools, such as long-handled tongs, spatulas, and basting brushes, can make grilling more efficient and safer. Avoid using forks to turn meat, as they pierce the food and let precious juices escape, leading to dry results. Proper tools help you handle food more effectively and maintain its integrity.

Seasoning food improperly or insufficiently is another pitfall. While marinades and rubs add flavor, don't forget to season with salt and pepper appropriately. Salt enhances the natural flavors and helps create a crust on grilled meats. Be generous but balanced in your seasoning approach to ensure each bite is flavorful.

Forgetting to lubricate the grates can cause food to stick. Before placing food on the grill, oil the grates using a paper towel dipped in oil and held with tongs. This creates a non-stick surface, making it easier to flip and remove food without tearing.

Not considering the weather can also impact your grilling. Wind and cold can affect grill temperature and cooking times. Be prepared to adjust cooking times and fuel usage based on weather conditions. Wind can cause uneven heating, while cold temperatures might require a longer preheat time and more fuel to maintain the desired cooking temperature.

Finally, not experimenting and learning from mistakes can limit your growth as a griller. Every grill and cut of meat is different, and part of mastering grilling is understanding these nuances. Keep a grilling journal, noting what worked and what didn't for future reference. Embrace each grilling session as an opportunity to refine your skills and try new techniques.

Avoiding these common grilling mistakes will set you on the path to becoming a more proficient and confident griller. Each tip, from preheating the grill to proper seasoning, plays a crucial role in achieving delicious and consistent results. By paying attention to these details, you'll not only improve the quality of your food but also enhance the overall grilling experience for yourself and your guests. Remember, the journey to becoming a grill master involves continual learning and practice. So fire up the grill, apply these insights, and enjoy the delicious rewards of your efforts. A successful grilling experience often hinges on preparation and attentiveness, both of which play a vital role in avoiding common mistakes. Mastering the grill requires more than just technical knowledge; it involves understanding the subtleties of the cooking process and adapting to various challenges. By honing these skills, you can elevate your grilling to new heights and consistently deliver mouthwatering meals.

Chapter 3

Marinades, Rubs, and Sauces

Understanding Flavors: Marinades vs. Rubs

One of the most delightful aspects of grilling is the opportunity to play with flavors, and two of the most effective techniques to enhance the taste of your grilled foods are marinades and rubs. Understanding the differences between these two methods, knowing when to use each one, and mastering their applications can transform your grilling from good to extraordinary.

Marinades are liquid solutions that infuse food with flavor and, in some cases, tenderize it. They usually consist of three main components: an acid (such as vinegar, citrus juice, or wine), oil, and various seasonings (herbs, spices, garlic, etc.). The acid works to break down muscle fibers, which can help tenderize tougher cuts of meat, while the oil helps to carry the flavors into the food and keep it moist.

Creating a balanced marinade is an art. Too much acid can make meat mushy, while too much oil can prevent the marinade from penetrating deeply. A good rule of thumb is to use a ratio of three parts oil to one part acid. For example, a simple marinade might include olive oil, lemon juice, minced garlic, and a blend of herbs like thyme and rosemary.

Timing is crucial when marinating. Delicate proteins like fish and seafood only need to marinate for 15 to

30 minutes, as their structure can break down quickly. Chicken and pork can benefit from a few hours in a marinade, while tougher cuts of beef, like flank steak or brisket, can be marinated overnight. Always marinate in the refrigerator to prevent bacterial growth, and discard the marinade after use, as it can harbor harmful bacteria from the raw meat.

Marinades are particularly effective for adding depth of flavor to meats that will be cooked quickly over high heat. Chicken breasts, for instance, can be transformed by a few hours in a citrus and herb marinade, emerging from the grill juicy and flavorful. Similarly, a robust marinade with soy sauce, ginger, and garlic can infuse flank steak with an Asian-inspired flavor profile that's perfect for grilling.

Rubs, on the other hand, are dry mixtures of spices, herbs, and sometimes sugar and salt, applied directly to the surface of the meat. Unlike marinades, rubs do not penetrate deeply into the meat. Instead, they form a flavorful crust on the exterior during cooking. The key to a great rub is balance and harmony among its components, ensuring that no single flavor overwhelms the others.

A basic rub might include equal parts salt, pepper, paprika, and brown sugar, with additional spices like cumin, garlic powder, and chili powder added to taste. The salt in the rub helps to draw moisture from the meat's surface, which then combines with the spices to form a savory crust as it cooks. The sugar in the rub caramelizes under the heat, adding a subtle sweetness and helping to create a beautiful, rich color.

Rubs are particularly well-suited for meats that benefit from a beautifully charred exterior, like ribs, pork shoulder, or brisket. For example, a classic barbecue rub with paprika, brown sugar, garlic powder, and mustard powder can create a delectable crust on slow-cooked pork ribs, enhancing their smoky, savory flavor.

When applying a rub, it's important to coat the meat evenly and allow it to sit for at least 30 minutes before grilling, which gives the flavors a chance to meld with the meat's surface. For even more intense flavor, you can apply the rub the night before and let the meat rest in the refrigerator.

Understanding when to use a marinade versus a rub depends largely on the type of meat and the desired outcome. Marinades are ideal for imparting moisture and flavor to lean cuts of meat that might otherwise dry out on the grill. They're also great for tenderizing tougher cuts. Rubs, meanwhile, are perfect for creating a flavorful, textured crust on meats that benefit from a longer, slower cooking process or a quick, high-heat sear.

Experimentation is a key part of mastering marinades and rubs. Don't be afraid to mix and match ingredients to create your own signature flavors. For instance, try a yogurt-based marinade with garlic, lemon, and mint for lamb, or a coffee and cocoa rub for beef brisket to add a unique depth of flavor.

The balance of flavors in both marinades and rubs can also be influenced by cultural and regional preferences. Exploring these can open up a world of new tastes and techniques. For example, a traditional

Mexican adobo marinade, with its blend of vinegar, garlic, oregano, and chili peppers, can bring a vibrant, spicy note to grilled chicken or pork. Similarly, a North African-inspired rub with cumin, coriander, and cinnamon can add a warm, aromatic flavor to lamb or beef.

While marinades and rubs are powerful tools on their own, they can also be used in combination for a layering of flavors. Marinate your meat first to tenderize and infuse it with flavor, then apply a rub just before grilling to create a flavorful crust. This technique works particularly well with larger cuts of meat that will be cooked over a longer period, such as pork shoulder or beef brisket.

In addition to meats, both marinades and rubs can be used effectively with vegetables, enhancing their natural flavors and adding complexity. A balsamic marinade with garlic and rosemary can elevate grilled portobello mushrooms, while a spice rub with cumin and paprika can give grilled corn a smoky, savory kick.

To ensure the best results, always start with high-quality ingredients. Fresh herbs and spices will provide more vibrant flavors than their dried counterparts, and using good-quality oils and acids in your marinades will make a noticeable difference in the final dish.

Finally, remember that grilling is as much about joy and creativity as it is about technique. Enjoy the process of experimenting with different flavors and discovering what combinations work best for you. Whether you're marinating a piece of chicken or rubbing down a rack of ribs, each step is an opportunity to infuse your food with your own personal touch.

Understanding the differences between marinades and rubs, and mastering their use, will undoubtedly elevate your grilling game. Each method has its unique benefits and applications, and knowing how to use them effectively can lead to consistently delicious results. So, fire up your grill, gather your ingredients, and enjoy the flavorful journey that lies ahead. With practice and creativity, you'll soon be creating grilled dishes that are not only mouthwatering but also a true reflection of your culinary style. As you delve deeper into the world of marinades and rubs, it's important to appreciate how these techniques can be tailored to different cuisines and culinary traditions. Each culture brings its own unique blend of spices, herbs, and ingredients to the table, offering endless opportunities to experiment and innovate.

Creating Your Own Marinades

Creating your own marinades is a rewarding practice that allows you to infuse your culinary creations with a distinct personal touch. Marinades are versatile and can be tailored to suit any type of meat, seafood, or vegetable. By understanding the fundamental components and mastering the balance of flavors, you can transform ordinary dishes into extraordinary meals.

A well-crafted marinade generally consists of three main components: an acid, an oil, and seasonings. The acid, which could be vinegar, citrus juice, wine, or yogurt, serves to tenderize the meat by breaking down its fibers. The oil, such as olive oil or sesame oil, helps to keep the meat moist and acts as a carrier for the seasonings, ensuring they penetrate deeply. Seasonings, which include herbs, spices, garlic, and other flavorings, are what give the marinade its distinctive taste.

To begin creating your own marinades, it's helpful to start with a basic framework and then experiment with different ingredients to find the combinations you enjoy most. A simple yet effective marinade might include three parts oil to one part acid, with a handful of seasonings to taste. For example, a classic Mediterranean marinade could consist of olive oil, lemon juice, minced garlic, and a mix of dried oregano and rosemary.

The choice of acid in your marinade can greatly influence the flavor profile. Citrus juices like lemon, lime, and orange provide a bright, tangy flavor and are excellent for lighter meats such as chicken or fish. Vinegars, including balsamic, apple cider, and red wine vinegar, offer a more robust acidity that pairs well with red meats and heartier vegetables. Yogurt and buttermilk, with their creamy texture and mild tang, are particularly good for tenderizing tougher cuts of meat like lamb or beef.

Oils in marinades not only help distribute the flavors evenly but also add richness and moisture. Olive oil is a popular choice due to its mild flavor and health benefits. For an Asian-inspired twist, sesame oil can add a nutty depth, while coconut oil brings a subtle sweetness that complements tropical flavors. It's important to choose an oil that complements the other ingredients in your marinade to create a harmonious blend.

Seasonings are where you can truly let your creativity shine. Fresh herbs like basil, cilantro, and parsley add vibrant, aromatic notes, while dried herbs such as thyme, oregano, and sage provide a more concentrated flavor. Spices like cumin, paprika, and coriander can add warmth and complexity, while crushed garlic, ginger, and chilies can bring a punch of intensity. Don't be afraid to experiment with different combinations to find what works best for you.

Balancing the flavors in your marinade is crucial. Too much acid can make the meat mushy, while too much oil can prevent the flavors from penetrating deeply. A good starting point is to use a ratio of three parts oil to one part acid and then adjust to taste. You can always add a bit more acid or oil if needed, but it's harder to correct the balance once the meat has been marinating for a while.

Timing is another important factor when marinating. The length of time you should marinate depends on the type of meat and the strength of the marinade. Delicate proteins like fish and shellfish require only 15 to 30 minutes, as their structure breaks down quickly. Chicken and pork can benefit from a few hours in the marinade, while tougher cuts of beef and lamb can be left overnight. Always marinate in the refrigerator to prevent bacterial growth and maintain food safety.

To enhance the marinating process, consider using a resealable plastic bag or a glass container. These options allow the marinade to surround the meat completely, ensuring even coverage. Occasionally turning the meat while it's marinating can also help the flavors to permeate more evenly.

Once you've mastered the basics, you can start to explore more complex marinades. For instance, an Asian marinade might include soy sauce, rice vinegar, sesame oil, ginger, and garlic, providing a savory umami flavor that's perfect for beef or chicken. A Mexican-inspired marinade could feature lime juice, olive oil, cilantro, cumin, and jalapeño, adding a zesty, spicy kick to pork or seafood.

Cultural cuisines offer endless inspiration for marinade experimentation. Indian marinades often use yogurt, lemon juice, and a blend of spices like turmeric, cumin, and coriander to create richly flavored and tender dishes. Middle Eastern marinades might combine olive oil, lemon juice, garlic, and sumac, imparting a tangy, earthy taste to lamb or chicken. By exploring different culinary traditions, you can discover new flavor combinations and expand your marinade repertoire.

In addition to meats, marinades can also elevate the flavor of vegetables. Firm vegetables like zucchini, bell peppers, and eggplant can benefit from a brief soak in a marinade before grilling, roasting, or baking. A simple balsamic vinegar and olive oil marinade with a touch of garlic and herbs can transform these vegetables into a flavorful side dish. Even softer vegetables like mushrooms and tomatoes can be marinated for a short time to enhance their natural flavors.

When creating marinades, it's essential to consider
the end use of the marinated food. Some marinades
can double as basting sauces during cooking, while
others may need to be discarded due to raw meat
exposure. If you plan to use the marinade as a sauce,
set aside a portion before adding the meat, ensuring it
remains uncontaminated. Alternatively, you can boil
the used marinade to kill any bacteria and then use it
as a sauce or glaze.

Experimentation is key to finding the perfect
marinade for your taste. Keep a notebook to record
your marinade recipes, noting the ingredients and
proportions used, as well as the results. This practice
will help you refine your recipes over time and
develop a repertoire of go-to marinades for different
occasions.

Sharing your marinade creations with friends and
family is a wonderful way to gather feedback and
enjoy the fruits of your labor. Hosting a barbecue or
dinner party allows you to showcase your culinary
skills and experiment with different marinade
combinations. Encourage your guests to share their
thoughts and preferences, as this can provide valuable
insights for future experiments.

Creating your own marinades is an art that combines
science, creativity, and a love for good food. By
understanding the basic components and
experimenting with different ingredients, you can
develop a unique palette of flavors that reflect your
personal taste and culinary style. Whether you're
preparing a simple weeknight meal or a gourmet feast,
a well-crafted marinade can elevate your dishes and
delight your taste buds. So, gather your ingredients,

start experimenting, and enjoy the journey of creating delicious, flavorful marinades that will make your meals unforgettable. Marinades don't just enhance the flavor of your food—they also provide an opportunity to explore and appreciate a wide variety of ingredients and techniques. As you become more comfortable with creating your own marinades, you can begin to explore advanced techniques and ingredients that can further elevate your culinary creations.

Mastering Dry Rubs

Dry rubs are an essential tool in the culinary world, offering a straightforward yet profoundly impactful way to elevate the flavor of meats and vegetables. Composed solely of dry ingredients, they provide a concentrated burst of taste and aroma without the extra moisture found in marinades. Mastering dry rubs requires an understanding of how different spices and herbs interact, as well as the delicate balance between sweetness, saltiness, and heat.

At the core of an effective dry rub is a balance of four primary components: salt, sugar, heat, and aromatic spices. Each plays a critical role in developing the flavor profile of the dish. Salt enhances the natural flavors of the food and helps to tenderize meat by drawing out moisture and creating a brine-like effect. Sugar, often in the form of brown sugar due to its molasses content, adds a caramelized sweetness that balances spiciness and creates a beautiful crust when cooked. Heat elements, such as chili powder, cayenne pepper, or paprika, introduce varying levels of spiciness, while aromatic spices like cumin, coriander, and garlic powder add depth and complexity.

Creating a dry rub starts with selecting a base. Salt is non-negotiable; whether you choose kosher salt, sea salt, or smoked salt, it forms the foundation. For sweetness, brown sugar is a popular choice due to its moisture content and ability to create a caramelized crust. However, other sugars like granulated white sugar, turbinado sugar, or even maple sugar can offer unique twists. The heat component can be adjusted to suit your preference, ranging from mild paprika to intense cayenne pepper. Aromatic spices are where creativity can truly shine, allowing you to experiment with different flavor profiles.

A classic barbecue rub, for instance, might include equal parts kosher salt and brown sugar, with additions of paprika, black pepper, cumin, garlic powder, onion powder, and cayenne pepper. This blend delivers a balanced sweetness, a hint of heat, and a depth of flavor that complements pork, beef, and chicken alike. For a Mediterranean twist, you might combine kosher salt with dried oregano, thyme, garlic powder, and lemon zest, creating a vibrant and herbaceous rub perfect for lamb or chicken.

The process of applying a dry rub is straightforward but requires attention to detail. Begin by patting the meat dry with paper towels to remove any excess moisture, ensuring the rub adheres properly. Generously sprinkle the rub over the meat, then use your hands to massage it in, ensuring even coverage. Some chefs recommend letting the seasoned meat rest for a while, allowing the flavors to penetrate the surface. This resting period can range from a few minutes to several hours, depending on the type of meat and your desired intensity of flavor.

Cooking methods can also influence the effectiveness of a dry rub. Grilling, smoking, and roasting are particularly well-suited, as the high heat helps to develop a flavorful crust. When grilling, for example, the direct heat caramelizes the sugars in the rub, creating a deliciously charred exterior. Smoking, on the other hand, allows the spices to infuse slowly into the meat, resulting in a complex, smoky flavor. Roasting in the oven can also yield excellent results, particularly for larger cuts of meat like roasts or whole chickens.

Vegetables can also benefit from the application of a dry rub. Root vegetables like potatoes, carrots, and sweet potatoes absorb flavors well and develop a delightful crust when roasted. For a simple yet flavorful vegetable rub, consider a mix of kosher salt, smoked paprika, garlic powder, and dried thyme. Toss the vegetables in olive oil first to help the rub adhere, then roast them at a high temperature until tender and caramelized.

Experimentation is key to mastering dry rubs. Don't be afraid to try new combinations and adjust the ratios to suit your taste. Keep a notebook to record your experiments, noting the ingredients, proportions, and results. This practice will help you refine your recipes over time and develop a repertoire of go-to rubs for different types of dishes.

Beyond the basics, there are countless ways to elevate your dry rubs. Consider incorporating non-traditional ingredients like coffee grounds, cocoa powder, or ground nuts to add unique flavors and textures. Coffee grounds, for instance, add a deep, earthy bitterness that pairs beautifully with beef. Cocoa powder can introduce a subtle richness and complexity, particularly in conjunction with chili powder for a Mexican-inspired rub. Ground nuts like almonds or pecans can add a nutty crunch, enhancing both flavor and texture.

Cultural influences can also inspire new and exciting dry rub combinations. For a Caribbean-inspired rub, combine kosher salt with allspice, cinnamon, nutmeg, thyme, and scotch bonnet pepper. This blend delivers a warm, spicy-sweet flavor perfect for chicken or pork. An Indian-inspired rub might feature a mix of kosher salt, turmeric, cumin, coriander, garam masala, and chili powder, creating a vibrant and aromatic blend ideal for lamb or fish.

When developing your own dry rubs, it's important to consider the end use. Some rubs are best suited for short cooking times, while others can withstand longer, slower methods. For instance, a rub with a high sugar content might burn if exposed to direct high heat for too long, whereas a rub focused on herbs and spices can handle extended smoking or roasting.

Storage is another important aspect of mastering dry rubs. Keep your rubs fresh by storing them in airtight containers away from light and heat. Mason jars or resealable plastic bags work well for this purpose. Label each container with the date and ingredients to keep track of your creations and ensure you're using them at their peak flavor.

Sharing your dry rub creations with friends and family can be a rewarding experience. Host a barbecue or dinner party to showcase your favorite rubs and gather feedback. This social aspect not only allows you to enjoy the fruits of your labor but also provides valuable insights that can help you refine your recipes further.

Mastering dry rubs is a journey of exploration and creativity. By understanding the fundamental components and experimenting with different ingredients and techniques, you can develop a unique palette of flavors that reflect your personal taste and culinary style. Whether you're grilling, smoking, roasting, or even sautéing, a well-crafted dry rub can transform your dishes and delight your taste buds. So, gather your spices, start experimenting, and enjoy the process of creating delicious, flavorful dry rubs that will make your meals unforgettable. As you delve deeper into the world of dry rubs, you'll discover that the possibilities are virtually endless. Each ingredient you add brings its own unique character, and the way these flavors meld together can produce surprising and delightful results. Pay attention to how different spices and herbs interact—not just with the food, but with each other. Some combinations may enhance the overall flavor, while others might clash or overpower more delicate notes.

Classic Barbecue Sauces

The allure of classic barbecue sauces lies in their ability to transform simple grilled or smoked meats into something extraordinary. Each region in the

United States, and indeed the world, has its own unique take on barbecue sauce, reflecting local ingredients, traditions, and tastes. Mastering these sauces opens up a world of flavor possibilities, each bringing its own story to the table.

Kansas City-style barbecue sauce is perhaps the most iconic. Thick, sweet, and tangy, it's a favorite for ribs and pulled pork. The base of this sauce is typically ketchup, which provides a rich, tomatoey foundation. Brown sugar or molasses adds the characteristic sweetness, while vinegar balances it with acidity. Spices like chili powder, paprika, and garlic powder give it depth and complexity. To make a classic Kansas City sauce, simmer ketchup, brown sugar, apple cider vinegar, molasses, and a blend of spices until it thickens into a luscious, sticky glaze.

Memphis-style barbecue sauce is less sweet and more tangy, often with a bit of heat. This sauce relies on a tomato base as well, but it's typically thinner than its Kansas City counterpart. Vinegar plays a prominent role, giving the sauce a sharp, tangy flavor that cuts through the richness of pork. To prepare a Memphis-style sauce, combine tomato sauce, apple cider vinegar, Worcestershire sauce, and a pinch of cayenne pepper for heat. Simmer until the flavors meld, creating a sauce that pairs beautifully with smoked meats.

South Carolina mustard sauce is a departure from the tomato-based sauces, using yellow mustard as its base. This sauce is tangy and slightly sweet, with a unique flavor profile that complements pork, particularly pulled pork sandwiches. To make this distinctive sauce, start with yellow mustard and add apple cider vinegar, brown sugar, honey, and a touch of hot sauce. Simmer gently to blend the flavors. The result is a bright, golden sauce that adds a tangy kick to your barbecue.

Alabama white sauce stands out with its creamy, mayonnaise base. This sauce is a staple in Northern Alabama and is traditionally served with smoked chicken. The tanginess of vinegar and the bite of horseradish cut through the richness of the mayonnaise, creating a balanced and flavorful sauce. To prepare Alabama white sauce, whisk together mayonnaise, apple cider vinegar, lemon juice, prepared horseradish, and a touch of black pepper. This sauce is best used as a finishing touch, brushed onto grilled or smoked chicken right before serving.

Texas-style barbecue sauce often takes a backseat to the meat itself, especially brisket, which is the star of Texan barbecue. When sauce is used, it's typically a thinner, more savory concoction. This sauce usually starts with beef broth or drippings, combined with tomato paste, Worcestershire sauce, and a hint of cumin and chili powder. To make a Texas-style sauce, simmer beef broth, tomato paste, Worcestershire sauce, and spices until it reduces slightly. This sauce enhances the flavor of the meat without overpowering it.

North Carolina is known for its vinegar-based sauces, which are perfect for cutting through the fatty richness of pork. There are two main types: Eastern and Western (or Lexington-style) North Carolina sauces. Eastern North Carolina sauce is very simple, consisting mainly of vinegar, a touch of sugar, salt, and red pepper flakes. This thin, spicy sauce is typically used as a mop sauce during cooking and as a finishing sauce. To make it, combine apple cider vinegar, a bit of white sugar, salt, and red pepper flakes, and let it sit to meld the flavors.

Western North Carolina sauce, also known as Lexington-style, adds a touch of tomato to the vinegar base, usually in the form of ketchup or tomato sauce. This slight tomato addition gives it a bit more body and sweetness while retaining the signature tanginess. To prepare this sauce, mix apple cider vinegar, ketchup, brown sugar, and red pepper flakes, and simmer briefly to blend the flavors.

While these classic sauces provide a solid foundation, the beauty of barbecue lies in experimentation and personalization. Each cook can adjust the ingredients to suit their taste, adding more heat, sweetness, or tanginess as desired. The key is to start with a balanced base and tweak it incrementally, tasting as you go.

To elevate your barbecue sauces, consider incorporating some advanced techniques and ingredients. Smoking your sauce can add an extra layer of depth and complexity. To do this, prepare your sauce as usual, then place it in a shallow pan and set it in your smoker for 30 to 60 minutes, stirring occasionally. The smoke will infuse the sauce with a rich, smoky flavor that complements the grilled or smoked meat perfectly.

Another way to enhance your sauces is by using fresh ingredients whenever possible. Fresh onions, garlic, and herbs can make a significant difference in flavor compared to their dried counterparts. Sautéing onions and garlic before adding them to your sauce can also bring out their natural sweetness and depth.

For those who enjoy a bit of experimentation, try adding unique ingredients to your sauces. A splash of bourbon or whiskey can add a warm, caramel-like flavor to sweet sauces. Fresh fruit, such as peaches or mangoes, can be pureed and added for a touch of natural sweetness and acidity. Spices like star anise or cinnamon can add unexpected depth and complexity.

Balancing flavors is crucial in barbecue sauces. If a sauce is too sweet, a splash of vinegar or a squeeze of lemon juice can brighten it up. If it's too tangy, a bit more sugar or honey can round it out. Heat can be adjusted with different types of peppers or hot sauces depending on your preference.

Storing barbecue sauces properly is also important to maintain their flavor and safety. Most homemade sauces will keep in the refrigerator for up to a week in an airtight container. Some sauces, particularly those high in vinegar and sugar, may last longer. For longer storage, consider freezing your sauces in small portions so you can defrost only what you need.

Sharing barbecue sauces with friends and family can be a joyous experience. Bottling your homemade sauces in decorative jars and giving them as gifts can introduce others to the flavors you've perfected. Including a recipe card with ingredients and suggested uses makes the gift even more special.

Classic barbecue sauces are more than just condiments; they are an integral part of the barbecue experience. By understanding the nuances of each style and experimenting with your own variations, you can create sauces that elevate your barbecue to new heights. Whether you're grilling in your backyard or preparing for a big family gathering, the right barbecue sauce can make all the difference. Embrace the tradition, savor the process, and enjoy the delicious results of your efforts. In addition to the classic barbecue sauces mentioned, there are several lesser-known but equally delicious regional sauces worth exploring. These sauces bring unique flavors and ingredients to the table, offering a broader palette for your barbecue adventures.

Innovative Sauces and Glazes

Creating innovative sauces and glazes can elevate your culinary creations to new heights, adding layers of flavor that can transform a simple dish into something extraordinary. Whether you're working with grilled meats, roasted vegetables, or even desserts, the right sauce or glaze can make all the difference. This chapter explores the art of crafting unique and inventive sauces and glazes that will inspire your cooking and delight your taste buds.

One of the keys to creating innovative sauces is to think beyond the traditional ingredients and flavor profiles. For instance, incorporating unexpected fruits, herbs, and spices can result in a sauce that is both surprising and delicious. Imagine a blueberry-balsamic reduction, where the tartness of the berries is balanced by the acidity of the vinegar, creating a complex and slightly sweet glaze perfect for duck or pork. To make this sauce, combine fresh blueberries, balsamic vinegar, a touch of honey, and a pinch of salt in a saucepan. Simmer until the blueberries break down and the mixture thickens, then strain to remove the solids for a smooth, glossy glaze.

Another approach to innovation is to draw inspiration from global cuisines. Many cultures have their own unique sauces and glazes that can be adapted and incorporated into your repertoire. For example, a Thai-inspired peanut sauce can add a rich, nutty flavor to grilled chicken or tofu. To make this sauce, blend together peanut butter, coconut milk, soy sauce, lime juice, garlic, ginger, and a bit of brown sugar. Adjust the consistency with water or more coconut milk as needed. This versatile sauce can also be used as a dip for vegetables or as a dressing for noodle salads.

For a Mediterranean twist, consider a pomegranate molasses glaze. Pomegranate molasses, with its deep, tangy sweetness, pairs beautifully with lamb, chicken, or roasted vegetables. To create this glaze, mix pomegranate molasses with a touch of honey, lemon juice, and a pinch of cinnamon. Brush it onto your meat or vegetables during the last few minutes of cooking, allowing it to caramelize and form a glossy coating.

Herbs and spices are another avenue for innovation. A sauce infused with fresh herbs can bring a burst of brightness to your dishes. Try a chimichurri sauce, a staple of Argentinian cuisine, which is vibrant and herbaceous. Combine finely chopped parsley, cilantro, garlic, red wine vinegar, olive oil, and a touch of red pepper flakes. This sauce is traditionally served with grilled steak, but it's equally delicious on chicken, fish, or even drizzled over roasted vegetables.

For a more exotic flavor, experiment with a Moroccan-inspired charmoula sauce. This North African sauce combines fresh herbs with warm spices and preserved lemon for a complex and aromatic condiment. To make charmoula, blend together cilantro, parsley, garlic, cumin, paprika, preserved lemon, olive oil, and a touch of salt. This sauce is perfect for marinating fish or chicken before grilling or as a finishing touch for roasted vegetables.

In the realm of glazes, the balance between sweet and savory is crucial. A miso-honey glaze, for instance, brings together the umami richness of miso with the sweetness of honey, creating a glaze that is perfect for salmon or roasted root vegetables. To prepare this glaze, whisk together white miso paste, honey, soy sauce, and a bit of rice vinegar. Brush it onto your protein or vegetables during the last few minutes of cooking, allowing it to caramelize without burning.

For dessert, innovative sauces can add a surprising twist to classic sweets. A salted caramel sauce, for example, can elevate a simple scoop of vanilla ice cream or a slice of apple pie. To make salted caramel, melt sugar in a saucepan until it turns a deep amber color, then carefully whisk in heavy cream, butter, and a generous pinch of sea salt. The result is a rich, buttery sauce with a perfect balance of sweet and salty.

Chocolate lovers might enjoy a spicy chocolate sauce, combining the richness of dark chocolate with the warmth of chili peppers. Melt dark chocolate with a bit of heavy cream, then stir in a pinch of cayenne pepper or chili powder. This sauce can be drizzled over brownies, used as a dip for fresh fruit, or even stirred into hot coffee for a spicy mocha.

When creating innovative sauces and glazes, it's important to consider the texture and consistency. A sauce that is too thin can run off your food, while one that is too thick can overwhelm it. Thickeners like cornstarch, arrowroot, or even a reduction technique can help achieve the perfect consistency. For example, a red wine reduction sauce can add elegance to a steak dinner. Simply simmer red wine with shallots, garlic, and a sprig of thyme until it reduces by half, then whisk in a bit of butter for richness and shine.

Acidity is another critical element in crafting balanced sauces. Vinegars, citrus juices, and fermented ingredients can provide the necessary tang to cut through rich flavors. A tamarind glaze, for example, brings a unique sour note that pairs beautifully with grilled meats. To make this glaze, combine tamarind paste with brown sugar, soy sauce, garlic, and a bit of water. Simmer until it thickens, then brush onto your meat during the last few minutes of cooking.

Experimentation is at the heart of innovation. Don't be afraid to play with different ingredients and techniques to discover new flavor combinations. A blackberry-ginger glaze, for instance, combines the tartness of blackberries with the zing of fresh ginger. Simmer blackberries with grated ginger, honey, and a splash of red wine vinegar until the berries break down and the mixture thickens. This glaze is excellent on grilled pork chops or as a finishing touch for roasted duck.

Seasonal ingredients can also inspire innovative sauces. In the summer, a fresh tomato and basil sauce can capture the essence of the season. Simply sauté ripe tomatoes with garlic and olive oil until they break down into a chunky sauce, then stir in fresh basil leaves and a pinch of salt. This sauce is perfect for pasta, grilled chicken, or as a topping for bruschetta.

In the fall, a pear and sage glaze can bring warmth and depth to your dishes. Simmer diced pears with fresh sage, apple cider, and a touch of maple syrup until the pears are soft and the mixture has thickened. This glaze pairs beautifully with roasted pork or chicken, adding a sweet and herbal note that complements the savory flavors.

Finally, presentation matters as much as flavor. A beautifully drizzled sauce or a perfectly glazed piece of meat can make your dish look as good as it tastes. Use squeeze bottles for precise drizzling, or a brush for even glazing. Garnish with fresh herbs, citrus zest, or a sprinkle of sea salt to add visual appeal and an extra layer of flavor.

Innovative sauces and glazes are about pushing boundaries and exploring new culinary horizons. By combining unexpected ingredients, drawing inspiration from global cuisines, and paying attention to balance and texture, you can create sauces that not only enhance your dishes but also tell a story. Embrace the creativity and experimentation that comes with crafting these sauces, and you'll find yourself discovering new favorites that add excitement and depth to your cooking. Innovative sauces and glazes can also make ordinary meals feel special, even when you're pressed for time. Quick and easy sauces that pack a flavor punch are invaluable for weeknight dinners or last-minute gatherings. For instance, a quick lemon-caper sauce can turn a simple grilled fish into a gourmet dish. To make it, melt a bit of butter in a pan, then add minced garlic and cook until fragrant. Stir in fresh lemon juice, capers, and a splash of white wine. Simmer for a few minutes to meld the flavors, and finish with chopped parsley for a bright, tangy accompaniment that complements seafood beautifully.

Marinade and Rub Application Tips

When it comes to elevating the flavor of your dishes, mastering the application of marinades and rubs is an essential skill. These techniques infuse your meats, seafood, and even vegetables with layers of complexity, transforming simple ingredients into culinary delights. Understanding how to apply marinades and rubs effectively can make a significant difference in the taste and texture of your food. This chapter delves into practical and actionable tips for beginners, helping you to maximize the potential of marinades and rubs in your cooking.

Marinades are liquid mixtures that typically include an acid (like vinegar or citrus juice), oil, and various herbs and spices. The acid helps to tenderize the meat by breaking down its proteins, while the oil carries flavor and moisture into the food. Spices and herbs add layers of taste. To make the most out of your marinades, it's crucial to balance these elements correctly.

When preparing a marinade, start by selecting the right acid. Different acids work better with different types of meat. For example, citrus juices such as lemon or lime are excellent for poultry and seafood, providing a bright, fresh flavor. Vinegars, like apple cider or balsamic, are versatile and work well with a variety of meats, including pork and beef. Yogurt, often used in Indian cuisine, not only tenderizes but also adds a creamy texture and subtle tanginess, making it perfect for chicken.

The next step is to choose your oil. Olive oil is a popular choice due to its rich flavor and health benefits, but you can also use other oils like sesame oil for an Asian twist or avocado oil for a neutral taste. The oil helps to distribute fat-soluble flavors from herbs and spices evenly across the meat.

Spices and herbs are where you can get creative. Fresh herbs like rosemary, thyme, and basil can add a burst of freshness, while dried spices such as cumin, coriander, and paprika provide depth and warmth. Don't be afraid to experiment with combinations to find your favorite flavor profiles. For a simple yet effective marinade, try mixing olive oil, lemon juice, garlic, rosemary, and black pepper for a classic and versatile option.

Once your marinade is prepared, it's time to apply it to your meat. Place your meat in a resealable plastic bag or a shallow dish, then pour the marinade over it, ensuring all surfaces are well-coated. If using a bag, squeeze out as much air as possible before sealing it to ensure the marinade is in full contact with the meat. For the best results, marinate in the refrigerator for at least 30 minutes to several hours, depending on the type of meat and desired flavor intensity. Seafood generally requires less time, often 30 minutes to an hour, while tougher cuts of meat like beef brisket can benefit from marinating overnight.

While marinating, periodically turn the meat to ensure even distribution of the marinade. However, avoid marinating for too long, as the acid can eventually break down the meat too much, leading to a mushy texture. For most meats, 24 hours is the maximum recommended marinating time.

Rubs, on the other hand, are dry mixtures of spices, herbs, salt, and sometimes sugar, designed to coat the exterior of the meat. Unlike marinades, rubs form a flavorful crust when cooked, adding texture and an intense burst of flavor. The key to a great rub is balance and even application.

To create a balanced rub, start with a base of salt and sugar. Salt enhances the meat's natural flavors and helps to draw out moisture, forming a brine that keeps the meat juicy. Sugar, when exposed to heat, caramelizes and forms a delicious crust. Brown sugar is a common choice due to its rich, molasses-like flavor, but white sugar or even honey powder can be used for different effects.

Next, add your spices. Paprika, garlic powder, onion powder, and black pepper are classics that provide a robust foundation. From there, you can customize with additional spices like chili powder for heat, cumin for earthiness, or mustard powder for a tangy kick. Freshly ground spices generally offer more intense flavors compared to pre-ground ones.

When applying a rub, ensure your meat is dry. Pat it down with paper towels to remove excess moisture, which allows the rub to adhere better. Generously sprinkle the rub over the meat, then use your hands to massage it in, ensuring even coverage. Don't be afraid to be liberal with your rub; a thick coating will result in a more flavorful crust.

For larger cuts of meat, like a pork shoulder or brisket, consider applying the rub the night before cooking and letting it rest in the refrigerator. This allows the spices to penetrate deeper into the meat. For smaller cuts or quicker cooking meats, such as chicken breasts or steaks, applying the rub about 30 minutes before cooking is usually sufficient.

When cooking meat with a rub, be mindful of the heat. High heat can cause the sugar in the rub to burn, leading to a bitter taste. For grilling, consider using a two-zone fire, where one side of the grill is hotter than the other. Start the meat on the cooler side to cook through, then move it to the hotter side to sear and caramelize the exterior. This method helps prevent burning while still achieving a flavorful crust.

Combining marinades and rubs can also be a powerful technique. Marinating meat first to tenderize and infuse it with flavor, then applying a rub before cooking, can create a multi-layered taste experience. For example, marinate chicken thighs in a mixture of yogurt, lemon juice, and garlic, then apply a rub of cumin, coriander, and paprika before grilling. This approach ensures the meat is juicy and flavorful on the inside, with a bold, spicy crust on the outside.

When it comes to seafood, marinades and rubs can be equally transformative. For a simple yet flavorful fish marinade, mix olive oil, lemon juice, dill, and minced garlic. Marinate the fish for about 30 minutes before grilling or baking. For a rub, consider a blend of smoked paprika, garlic powder, and a touch of cayenne pepper. Apply it to shrimp or scallops for a smoky, spicy kick.

Vegetables can also benefit from marinades and rubs. Marinate portobello mushrooms in balsamic vinegar, olive oil, and thyme before grilling for a meaty, umami-rich flavor. Alternatively, coat cauliflower florets with a rub of turmeric, cumin, and chili powder before roasting for a vibrant and spicy side dish.

In the end, the success of marinades and rubs lies in understanding the balance of flavors and the proper application techniques. By experimenting with different ingredients and methods, you can discover combinations that suit your taste and enhance your cooking. Whether you're preparing a simple weeknight dinner or a special occasion feast, mastering these techniques will help you create dishes that are flavorful, tender, and unforgettable. Embrace the process, trust your instincts, and enjoy the culinary journey of transforming basic ingredients into extraordinary meals. One often overlooked aspect of using marinades and rubs is the importance of proper storage and handling. Ensuring that your meat is marinated or coated with a rub in a clean, food-safe environment is crucial to prevent contamination. Always use clean utensils and containers, and avoid cross-contamination between raw meat and other ingredients. If you plan to use the leftover marinade as a sauce, be sure to boil it thoroughly to kill any harmful bacteria.

Chapter 4

Grilling Beef

Selecting the Best Cuts of Beef

Choosing the right cut of beef can significantly impact the outcome of your dish, whether you're grilling, roasting, or slow-cooking. Understanding the characteristics of different beef cuts, including their texture, flavor, and best cooking methods, is essential for any home cook or aspiring chef. This chapter provides comprehensive guidance on selecting the best cuts of beef, ensuring you make informed decisions that enhance your culinary creations.

Beef is divided into primal cuts, which are then broken down into subprimal cuts and individual portions. The primary primal cuts include the chuck, rib, loin, round, flank, short plate, brisket, and shank. Each cut has unique attributes and is suitable for specific cooking techniques.

Starting with the chuck, this cut comes from the shoulder area of the cow. The chuck is known for its rich, beefy flavor and generous marbling, which makes it ideal for slow-cooking methods like braising and stewing. Popular cuts from the chuck include chuck roast, chuck steak, and the versatile ground chuck, perfect for making juicy burgers. When selecting chuck, look for a good balance of fat and meat, with even marbling throughout.

Moving to the rib section, this primal cut is prized for its tenderness and flavor. The rib primal includes the ribeye, one of the most sought-after steaks due to its intense marbling and succulent texture. Ribeye steaks are excellent for grilling or pan-searing. Another standout from this section is the prime rib, a luxurious roast that is perfect for special occasions. When choosing rib cuts, opt for meat with ample marbling and a bright, red color, indicating freshness.

The loin section is divided into the short loin and the sirloin. The short loin is home to some of the most tender and desirable cuts, such as the tenderloin (filet mignon), T-bone, and porterhouse steaks. These cuts are best suited for high-heat, quick-cooking methods like grilling, broiling, or searing. The sirloin, located just behind the short loin, offers a range of cuts that are flavorful and versatile, including the top sirloin and bottom sirloin. These cuts can be grilled, roasted, or used in stir-fries. When selecting loin cuts, look for fine-grained texture and even marbling.

The round primal, located at the rear of the cow, is known for its leanness and affordability. While not as tender as the rib or loin cuts, the round offers robust flavor and can be delicious when cooked properly. Common cuts from this section include the top round, bottom round, and eye of round. These cuts are best suited for roasting or braising. When choosing round cuts, look for a uniform, deep red color and minimal visible fat.

The flank, located just below the loin, is a long, flat cut known for its strong beefy flavor. Flank steak is popular for grilling and is often used in dishes like fajitas and stir-fries. It's essential to marinate flank steak to enhance its tenderness and flavor. When selecting flank steak, choose a piece with a consistent thickness and a rich color.

The short plate, found below the rib, is another flavorful, though tougher, section. This primal cut includes the skirt steak, known for its loose grain and intense beef flavor. Skirt steak is excellent for grilling or pan-searing and should be sliced against the grain to maximize tenderness. When selecting skirt steak, look for a piece with a uniform thickness and good marbling.

The brisket, located in the chest area, is renowned for its rich flavor and tenderness when cooked low and slow. This cut is ideal for smoking, braising, or slow roasting. Brisket is divided into two parts: the flat and the point. The flat is leaner and more uniform in shape, while the point is fattier and more flavorful. When choosing brisket, look for a piece with a good balance of fat and meat, and a bright, fresh color.

The shank, found in the leg, is one of the toughest cuts but also one of the most flavorful when cooked correctly. This cut is best suited for slow-cooking methods like braising, which breaks down the tough fibers and results in a tender, flavorful dish. Osso buco, a classic Italian dish, is made from the shank. When selecting shank, look for a piece with a good amount of connective tissue and a rich color.

In addition to understanding the primal cuts, it's important to know how to identify quality beef. When selecting any cut, consider the grade of the beef, which indicates the quality and marbling. The USDA grades beef as Prime, Choice, and Select. Prime grade has the most marbling and is the highest quality, making it ideal for grilling and other high-heat cooking methods. Choice grade has less marbling than Prime but is still very high quality and suitable for a variety of cooking techniques. Select grade has the least marbling and is best for slow-cooking methods to ensure tenderness.

When purchasing beef, pay attention to the color and texture of the meat. Fresh beef should have a bright, cherry-red color, indicating it has been properly aged and is not spoiled. The texture should be firm to the touch, with no slimy or sticky residue. The fat should be white or creamy-colored, not yellow or gray.

Proper storage of beef is also crucial to maintaining its quality. Store beef in the coldest part of your refrigerator and use it within a few days of purchase. If you need to store it longer, consider freezing it. Wrap the meat tightly in plastic wrap or aluminum foil, then place it in a freezer-safe bag to prevent freezer burn. Label the package with the date so you can keep track of how long it has been frozen.

Understanding the best cooking methods for each cut is essential to achieving the best results. Tender cuts like ribeye, tenderloin, and strip steak are best cooked quickly over high heat, while tougher cuts like chuck, brisket, and shank benefit from slow-cooking methods that break down connective tissue and render the meat tender and flavorful.

For example, a ribeye steak can be seasoned simply with salt and pepper, then grilled to medium-rare perfection, allowing the marbling to melt and infuse the meat with flavor. In contrast, a chuck roast should be seared to develop a rich crust, then braised with aromatic vegetables and broth for several hours until it becomes melt-in-your-mouth tender.

When cooking leaner cuts like the top round or eye of round, consider marinating them before cooking to add flavor and moisture. Roasting these cuts at a lower temperature can also help maintain their tenderness. For flank and skirt steaks, marinating and cooking them quickly over high heat, then slicing them thinly against the grain, will ensure they remain tender and flavorful.

By understanding the unique characteristics and best uses for each cut of beef, you can make informed decisions that enhance your cooking. Whether you're preparing a simple weeknight meal or a special occasion feast, selecting the right cut of beef and cooking it properly will ensure delicious, satisfying results. Embrace the variety and versatility of beef cuts, and enjoy exploring the endless possibilities they offer in your kitchen. Additionally, leveraging the knowledge of beef cuts allows you to manage your budget more effectively without compromising the quality and flavor of your meals. Often, the less expensive cuts, when prepared with the right techniques, can yield remarkably delicious dishes. For instance, cuts like the chuck roast, which might be overlooked in favor of pricier options, can transform into a hearty, flavorful pot roast with just a bit of patience and the right cooking method.

Preparing Beef for the Grill

Grilling beef is an art that combines the right cut, perfect seasoning, and proper technique to create a flavorful, juicy masterpiece. To ensure a successful grilling experience, one must understand the intricacies of selecting, preparing, and cooking beef. This chapter delves into the nuances of preparing beef for the grill, providing practical advice for beginners and seasoned grill masters alike.

Selecting the right cut of beef is the first crucial step. Not all cuts are ideal for grilling, so choosing wisely can make a significant difference. Popular choices for grilling include ribeye, strip steak, T-bone, porterhouse, sirloin, and flank steak. These cuts are known for their tenderness and robust flavor, making them perfect candidates for high-heat cooking methods. When selecting your beef, look for cuts with good marbling, as the intramuscular fat melts during grilling, enhancing the meat's flavor and juiciness.

Once you've selected your cut, the next step is to prepare the beef. Start by bringing the meat to room temperature, which ensures even cooking. Take the beef out of the refrigerator at least 30 minutes before grilling. This also allows the fibers to relax, contributing to a more tender result. While waiting, you can focus on seasoning.

Seasoning is a critical component in preparing beef for the grill. For many, a simple seasoning of kosher salt and freshly ground black pepper is sufficient. This classic combination highlights the beef's natural flavors. Generously season the meat on all sides, allowing the salt to penetrate and enhance the beef's taste. For those who enjoy experimenting, adding garlic powder, onion powder, or smoked paprika can introduce additional layers of flavor. If you prefer a more robust flavor profile, consider using a dry rub. A blend of spices like cumin, chili powder, brown sugar, and cayenne pepper can create a delicious crust on the beef, adding both taste and texture.

Marinades are another option for infusing flavor into your beef. Acidic marinades, which include ingredients like vinegar, citrus juice, or wine, can help tenderize tougher cuts such as flank steak. Combine these acids with oil, herbs, and spices to create a balanced marinade. Place the beef in a resealable plastic bag or a shallow dish, ensuring it is well-coated, and let it marinate in the refrigerator for at least 1-2 hours, or overnight for deeper flavor. Be mindful not to over-marinate, as the acids can break down the meat fibers too much, resulting in a mushy texture.

With your beef seasoned or marinated, it's time to focus on the grill. Preheating your grill is essential for achieving a good sear and cooking the meat evenly. For gas grills, preheat on high for about 10-15 minutes, ensuring the grates are hot. For charcoal grills, light the coals and wait until they are covered with a thin layer of gray ash, indicating they are ready. Clean the grill grates with a wire brush to remove any previous residue, then oil them lightly to prevent sticking.

Grilling involves both direct and indirect heat. Direct heat is used for searing the meat, creating those desirable grill marks and a flavorful crust. Indirect heat is for finishing the cooking process without burning the exterior while allowing the interior to reach the desired doneness. For thicker cuts like ribeye or porterhouse, start with direct heat to sear both sides, then move the beef to a cooler part of the grill to finish cooking. Thinner cuts, such as flank steak, can be cooked entirely over direct heat, given their shorter cooking time.

A crucial aspect of grilling is knowing when to flip the meat. Frequent flipping can prevent proper browning and searing. Aim to flip the beef only once during the cooking process. For a medium-rare steak, grill for about 4-5 minutes per side, depending on the thickness. Use a meat thermometer to ensure accuracy: 130-135°F for medium-rare, 140-145°F for medium, and 150-155°F for medium-well. Remember, the beef will continue to cook slightly after being removed from the grill due to residual heat.

Resting the meat after grilling is a step that should not be overlooked. Allow the beef to rest for at least 5-10 minutes before slicing. This resting period lets the juices redistribute throughout the meat, resulting in a more succulent and flavorful bite. Cutting into the beef too soon can cause the juices to run out, leaving the meat dry.

When it comes to slicing, especially for cuts like flank steak, it's important to cut against the grain. The grain refers to the direction of the muscle fibers. Slicing against the grain shortens these fibers, making the meat more tender and easier to chew. For thicker cuts, slicing the meat on a slight diagonal can also enhance the presentation and dining experience.

Pairing your grilled beef with complementary sides and sauces can elevate the meal. Classic accompaniments like grilled vegetables, baked potatoes, or a fresh salad balance the richness of the beef. For an added flavor boost, consider serving with compound butter, chimichurri, or a horseradish cream sauce. These additions can enhance the beef's natural flavors without overpowering them.

Safety is paramount when handling and grilling beef. Always use separate cutting boards and utensils for raw and cooked meat to avoid cross-contamination. Ensure your grill is placed in a well-ventilated area, away from any flammable materials. Keep a close eye on the grill while cooking to prevent flare-ups, which can char the meat and create a bitter taste.

Grilling beef is a skill that improves with practice. By understanding the nuances of selecting, preparing, and cooking beef on the grill, you can consistently achieve delicious results. Experiment with different cuts, seasonings, and techniques to find what works best for you. Whether you're a novice or an experienced griller, the satisfaction of serving perfectly grilled beef is well worth the effort. In addition to mastering the basics of grilling beef, it's worth exploring some advanced techniques that can further enhance your grilling repertoire. These methods can introduce new flavors and textures, providing a more diverse grilling experience.

Classic Beef Recipes: Burgers and Steaks

Few dishes encapsulate the essence of beef like a classic burger or a perfectly cooked steak. These staples of culinary tradition have countless variations and methods, yet the fundamentals remain the same. Crafting the ideal burger or steak involves selecting the right cut, mastering seasoning techniques, and employing precise cooking methods. This chapter explores the art of creating classic beef burgers and steaks, offering practical advice for beginners and seasoned cooks alike.

Burgers, a beloved comfort food, are deceptively simple yet require attention to detail to achieve perfection. The foundation of any great burger is the beef itself. Ground beef with a fat content of around 20% is ideal, typically labeled as 80/20. This ratio ensures a juicy, flavorful patty that retains moisture during cooking. Leaner cuts tend to dry out, while higher fat content can lead to excessive greasiness.

When forming your patties, avoid overworking the meat. Lightly shape the ground beef into patties slightly larger than the buns, as they will shrink during cooking. Press a small indentation in the center of each patty with your thumb. This prevents the burger from puffing up in the middle and ensures even cooking. Season the patties generously with salt and freshly ground black pepper just before cooking. Over-seasoning can mask the beef's natural flavor, so simplicity is key.

Cooking the perfect burger requires the right method. Grilling and pan-frying are two popular techniques. For grilling, preheat your grill to medium-high heat. Clean and oil the grates to prevent sticking. Place the patties on the grill and resist the urge to press them down with a spatula, as this squeezes out the flavorful juices. Cook for about 4-5 minutes per side for medium-rare, adjusting the time slightly for your desired doneness. For pan-frying, use a cast-iron skillet heated over medium-high heat. Add a small amount of oil and cook the patties similarly to the grilling method.

Cheese is a popular addition to burgers, and timing is crucial for optimal melting. Place a slice of cheese on each patty during the last minute of cooking. Covering the grill or pan with a lid helps the cheese melt evenly. Classic choices include cheddar, American, and Swiss, but feel free to experiment with blue cheese, pepper jack, or gouda for a unique twist.

Toasting the buns is a small step that makes a big difference. Lightly butter the cut sides and toast them on the grill or in the skillet until golden brown. This adds a pleasant crunch and prevents the buns from becoming soggy. Assemble your burger with fresh lettuce, ripe tomatoes, thinly sliced onions, and pickles. Condiments like ketchup, mustard, and mayonnaise are traditional, but aioli, barbecue sauce, and sriracha can add exciting flavors. Remember, the goal is to enhance, not overpower, the taste of the beef.

Steaks, on the other hand, are a celebration of beef in its purest form. Choosing the right cut is paramount. Ribeye, strip steak, filet mignon, and T-bone are revered for their tenderness and rich flavor. Look for steaks with good marbling, as the intramuscular fat melts during cooking, adding juiciness and depth of flavor.

Before cooking, bring the steaks to room temperature. This ensures even cooking from edge to center. Pat the steaks dry with paper towels to remove excess moisture, which helps achieve a better sear. Season generously with kosher salt and freshly ground black pepper. The salt draws out moisture, creating a flavorful crust when seared.

Searing is a critical step in cooking steaks. For a perfect sear, ensure your cooking surface is very hot. Whether using a grill or a cast-iron skillet, preheat it until it's smoking. Add a small amount of oil with a high smoke point, like canola or grapeseed oil. Place the steaks on the grill or in the skillet and avoid moving them until a crust forms. This typically takes about 2-3 minutes per side. For thicker steaks, sear the edges as well by holding them with tongs.

Cooking steaks to the desired doneness requires precision. Use a meat thermometer to check the internal temperature: 125°F for rare, 135°F for medium-rare, 145°F for medium, and 155°F for medium-well. After searing, you can finish cooking thicker steaks in the oven. Preheat the oven to 400°F, place the steaks on a baking sheet, and cook until they reach the desired temperature.

Resting steaks after cooking is essential. Allow them to rest for about 5-10 minutes. This resting period lets the juices redistribute, ensuring a moist and tender steak. Cutting into the steak too soon can cause the juices to escape, resulting in a dry texture.

Slicing the steak correctly enhances the eating experience. Always cut against the grain, which shortens the muscle fibers and makes the meat easier to chew. For cuts like flank or skirt steak, this step is especially important due to their naturally tougher texture.

Classic accompaniments for steaks include mashed potatoes, creamed spinach, and grilled asparagus. Sauces like béarnaise, chimichurri, and peppercorn sauce can elevate the dish. A pat of compound butter, made by mixing softened butter with herbs, garlic, and lemon zest, adds a luxurious finish when placed atop the resting steak.

Understanding the nuances of cooking burgers and steaks allows you to appreciate the versatility and depth of beef. Whether crafting a simple burger or a gourmet steak dinner, the key lies in quality ingredients, proper technique, and a love for the process. Experiment with different seasonings, cooking methods, and accompaniments to discover your personal preferences. The joy of mastering these classic beef recipes extends beyond the kitchen, bringing people together to share in the satisfaction of a meal well-prepared. The versatility of burgers and steaks also provides a fantastic opportunity to explore regional and international variations, each bringing its own unique twist to these classic dishes. Trying out these variations can not only expand your culinary skills but also introduce you to new flavors and cooking techniques.

Advanced Beef Recipes: Ribs and Brisket

Ribs and brisket, often revered as the pinnacle of beef barbecue, symbolize the essence of slow cooking and the celebration of deep, smoky flavors. These cuts demand patience, precision, and a bit of culinary intuition. Mastering ribs and brisket not only requires understanding the meat itself but also the techniques that transform these tougher cuts into tender, flavorful masterpieces. This chapter delves into the advanced world of beef ribs and brisket, offering practical, detailed guidance to help you achieve barbecue perfection.

Ribs, particularly beef short ribs, are prized for their rich, meaty flavor and succulent texture. The key to exceptional ribs lies in selecting the right cut and preparing it properly. Look for ribs with a good amount of marbling, as the fat will render during cooking, keeping the meat juicy and tender. Before cooking, remove the membrane from the underside of the ribs. This membrane can become tough and chewy, and its removal allows for better seasoning penetration.

Seasoning ribs is an art in itself. A balanced dry rub typically includes salt, pepper, paprika, garlic powder, onion powder, and a touch of brown sugar. The brown sugar helps to create a caramelized crust during cooking. Generously coat the ribs with the rub, pressing it into the meat to ensure it adheres well. For maximum flavor, let the seasoned ribs rest in the refrigerator for at least a couple of hours, or ideally overnight.

Smoking is the preferred method for cooking beef ribs, as it imparts a deep, smoky flavor that complements the richness of the meat. Begin by preheating your smoker to 225°F (107°C). Choose hardwoods like oak, hickory, or mesquite for a robust smoke flavor. Place the ribs in the smoker, bone side down, and cook low and slow. This process can take anywhere from 6 to 8 hours, depending on the size of the ribs and the consistency of your smoker's temperature. During smoking, it's crucial to maintain a steady temperature and avoid opening the smoker too often, as this can cause temperature fluctuations.

The hallmark of perfectly cooked ribs is when the meat is tender yet still clings to the bone. To achieve this, many pitmasters employ the Texas Crutch method, which involves wrapping the ribs in aluminum foil midway through the cooking process. This technique helps to speed up the cooking time and retain moisture. After about 3 to 4 hours of smoking, wrap the ribs tightly in foil with a splash of apple juice or beef broth to enhance moisture and flavor. Return the wrapped ribs to the smoker and continue cooking for another 2 to 3 hours.

Unwrap the ribs during the final hour of cooking to allow the bark to firm up. Brush on a thin layer of barbecue sauce if desired, though purists often enjoy their ribs with just the dry rub. The ribs are done when they reach an internal temperature of around 200°F (93°C) and a toothpick slides easily into the meat.

Brisket, another cornerstone of barbecue, presents its own set of challenges and rewards. This cut, taken from the breast or lower chest, is known for its toughness and requires slow cooking to break down the connective tissues. A whole packer brisket consists of two muscles: the flat, which is leaner, and the point, which is fattier and more flavorful. Selecting a brisket with good marbling and a flexible feel is crucial for achieving the best results.

Preparation begins with trimming the brisket. Remove any large, hard pieces of fat, leaving a thin layer to protect the meat during cooking. A classic Texas-style brisket rub is simple yet effective: equal parts kosher salt and coarse black pepper. Some variations include a bit of garlic powder or paprika, but the focus remains on enhancing the beef's natural flavor. Cover the brisket liberally with the rub, ensuring an even coating on all sides.

Smoking a brisket requires a low and slow approach similar to ribs. Preheat your smoker to 225°F (107°C) and use hardwoods like oak or pecan for a subtle, complementary smoke flavor. Place the brisket in the smoker with the fat side up, allowing the fat to render and baste the meat as it cooks. Maintain a steady temperature and avoid peeking too often, as consistency is key to breaking down the tough fibers and achieving tenderness.

The total cooking time for a brisket can range from 10 to 16 hours, depending on its size and the smoker's stability. As with ribs, many pitmasters use the Texas Crutch to help push the brisket through the stall—a phase where the internal temperature plateaus as the meat sweats out moisture. When the internal temperature reaches around 160°F (71°C), wrap the brisket tightly in butcher paper or aluminum foil and return it to the smoker. This step helps to retain moisture and accelerate cooking.

The brisket is done when it reaches an internal temperature of 200°F (93°C) to 205°F (96°C) and feels tender when probed. Once removed from the smoker, let the brisket rest, still wrapped, in a cooler or an insulated environment for at least an hour. This resting period allows the juices to redistribute, resulting in a juicy, flavorful brisket.

Slicing the brisket correctly is essential to showcasing your hard work. Separate the point from the flat by cutting along the natural seam of fat that divides them. Slice the flat against the grain into pencil-thick slices, and do the same with the point, though you can cut it into slightly thicker slices due to its higher fat content. Serve with classic sides like pickles, onions, and white bread, allowing the brisket's rich, smoky flavor to shine.

Perfecting ribs and brisket requires patience, practice, and a deep appreciation for the nuances of barbecue. Each step, from selecting the meat to seasoning, smoking, and slicing, contributes to the final product's success. These techniques, while demanding, offer immense rewards in flavor and satisfaction. As you become more comfortable with these advanced recipes, experiment with different rubs, wood types, and sauces to create your signature style. The journey to mastering ribs and brisket is as fulfilling as the mouthwatering results. Experimenting with different techniques and flavors allows you to continually refine your approach to ribs and brisket. One such technique involves playing with the type of wood you use for smoking. While oak and hickory are traditional choices, incorporating fruitwoods like apple or cherry can add a subtle sweetness and complexity to the meat. Combining different woods can create a unique flavor profile that distinguishes your barbecue from others.

Beef Cooking Times and Temperature Guide

Cooking beef to perfection hinges on understanding the delicate balance between time and temperature. This balance ensures that the meat is both safe to eat and reaches its desired tenderness and flavor. Different cuts of beef require distinct cooking methods, each with specific time and temperature guidelines. Mastering these elements will elevate your culinary skills and help you make the most out of every beef cut.

Beef is categorized into various primal cuts, which include the chuck, rib, loin, round, brisket, shank, and flank. Each of these cuts has unique characteristics that define how they should be cooked. For instance, tougher cuts like chuck and brisket benefit from slow cooking methods that break down their connective tissues, while tender cuts like ribeye and filet mignon are best suited for quick, high-temperature cooking.

Starting with steaks, the ideal cooking times and temperatures vary depending on the thickness of the cut and the desired level of doneness. For a medium-rare steak, which is often considered the gold standard, aim for an internal temperature of 130°F to 135°F (54°C to 57°C). A thick-cut ribeye or porterhouse, approximately 1.5 inches thick, should be seared over high heat for about 3-4 minutes per side and then finished in a preheated oven at 400°F (204°C) for an additional 5-7 minutes. For thinner cuts, like a New York strip, searing for 2-3 minutes per side might suffice without the need for oven finishing.

Cooking times for ground beef are crucial for safety, as it must be cooked to an internal temperature of at least 160°F (71°C) to eliminate harmful bacteria. Ground beef patties should be cooked over medium-high heat for 3-4 minutes per side, depending on thickness, until they reach this safe temperature. Using a meat thermometer is essential to ensure accuracy, as color alone is not a reliable indicator of doneness.

Roasts, such as prime rib or beef tenderloin, require a different approach. For a medium-rare prime rib, the goal is an internal temperature of 130°F to 135°F (54°C to 57°C). Begin by preheating your oven to 450°F (232°C), and roast the meat for 15 minutes to develop a flavorful crust. Then, reduce the oven temperature to 325°F (163°C) and continue roasting for approximately 13-15 minutes per pound. It's crucial to let the roast rest for at least 15 minutes after cooking to allow the juices to redistribute, ensuring a moist and tender result.

Beef tenderloin, known for its tenderness, should be cooked to an internal temperature of 125°F to 130°F (52°C to 54°C) for medium-rare. Sear the tenderloin on all sides in a hot skillet for about 2-3 minutes per side, then transfer it to a 400°F (204°C) oven for 20-25 minutes. As with other roasts, resting the meat after cooking is vital.

For tougher cuts like brisket and chuck, low and slow cooking methods are essential. Brisket should be cooked to an internal temperature of around 200°F to 205°F (93°C to 96°C) to break down the collagen and achieve a tender texture. This can be done in a smoker set to 225°F (107°C) and will take approximately 1.5

hours per pound. Wrapping the brisket in butcher paper or foil halfway through the cooking process can help retain moisture and speed up the cooking time.

Chuck roast, another tough cut, benefits from braising—a method that involves cooking the meat slowly in liquid. A chuck roast should be cooked at a low temperature of around 300°F (149°C) for 3-4 hours, or until it reaches an internal temperature of 195°F to 200°F (90°C to 93°C). This slow cooking process breaks down the tough fibers, resulting in a melt-in-your-mouth texture.

Short ribs, which are rich in flavor and marbling, also excel with slow cooking. Braising short ribs at 325°F (163°C) for about 2.5 to 3 hours, until they reach an internal temperature of around 200°F (93°C), will yield tender and flavorful meat. The braising liquid, often a mixture of beef broth, red wine, and aromatics, can be reduced and used as a sauce.

For a versatile and efficient method, sous vide cooking provides precise temperature control, ensuring perfect doneness throughout the meat. For steaks, set the sous vide water bath to 130°F (54°C) for medium-rare and cook for 1-4 hours, depending on the thickness. After sous vide cooking, a quick sear in a hot skillet will develop the desired crust.

Braising and slow roasting are ideal for tougher cuts like beef shank and oxtails. For braised beef shank, cook at 300°F (149°C) for 3-4 hours until the meat is tender and falls off the bone. Oxtails, rich in connective tissue and fat, should be braised at the same temperature for 3-4 hours, resulting in a deeply flavorful dish.

Flank steak, known for its robust flavor, should be cooked quickly at high heat to avoid toughness. For medium-rare, grill or broil the steak for about 4-5 minutes per side, aiming for an internal temperature of 130°F to 135°F (54°C to 57°C). Thinly slicing the steak against the grain is essential for maximum tenderness.

Beef ribs, whether short ribs or back ribs, benefit from slow smoking or braising. For smoked beef ribs, maintain a smoker temperature of 225°F (107°C) and cook until the internal temperature reaches 200°F to 205°F (93°C to 96°C), which can take 6-8 hours. Braising beef ribs at 325°F (163°C) for 2.5 to 3 hours will also achieve tender results.

Whether grilling, roasting, braising, or smoking, the key to perfect beef lies in understanding the specific time and temperature requirements for each cut. Consistently using a meat thermometer will ensure accuracy and help you achieve the desired level of doneness. Remember, the final resting period is just as crucial as the cooking process itself, allowing the juices to redistribute and ensuring a succulent, flavorful result.

By mastering these time and temperature guidelines, you'll be well-equipped to cook any cut of beef to perfection. Experimenting with different methods and cuts will enhance your culinary repertoire and deepen your appreciation for the nuances of beef cooking. Enjoy the process, savor the results, and share your culinary creations with those around you. To delve deeper into the subtleties of beef cooking, consider the role of marinating and seasoning, both of which can significantly influence cooking times and temperatures. Marinating, especially with acidic ingredients like vinegar or citrus, can tenderize tougher cuts and infuse them with additional flavors. However, it's important to adjust cooking times slightly, as the acid can begin breaking down the meat even before cooking starts.